BFI FILM CLASSICS

. . . .

Rob White
SERIES EDITOR

Edward Buscombe, Colin MacCabe and David Meeker
SERIES CONSULTANTS

Cinema is a fragile medium. Many of the great films now exist, if at all, in damaged or incomplete prints. Concerned about the deterioration in the physical state of our film heritage, the National Film and Television Archive, part of the British Film Institute's Collections Department, has compiled a list of 360 key works in the history of the cinema. The long-term goal of the Archive is to build a collection of perfect showprints of these films, which will then be screened regularly at the National Film Theatre in London in a year-round repertory.

BFI Film Classics is a series of books intended to introduce, interpret and honour these 360 films. Critics, scholars, novelists and those distinguished in the arts have been invited to write on a film of their choice, drawn from the Archive's list. The numerous illustrations have been made specially from the Archive's own prints.

With new titles published each year, the BFI Film Classics series is a unique, authoritative and highly readable guide to the masterpieces of world cinema.

The best movie publishing idea of the decade.
Philip French, *The Observer*

A remarkable series which does all kinds of varied and divergent things.
Michael Wood, *Sight and Sound*

Exquisitely dimensioned ... magnificently concentrated examples of freeform critical poetry.
Uncut

Alan Ladd, Jean Arthur, and Van Heflin

BFI FILM

CLASSICS

SHANE

. . . .

*Edward Countryman &
Evonne von Heussen-Countryman*

bfi Publishing

First published in 1999 by the
BRITISH FILM INSTITUTE
21 Stephen Street, London W1P 2LN

The British Film Institute
promotes greater understanding and
appreciation of, and access to, film and
moving image culture in the UK.

British Library Cataloguing-in-Publication Data
A catalogue record for this book is available from the British Library

ISBN 0–85170–732–7

Series design by
Andrew Barron & Collis Clements Associates

Typeset in Fournier and Franklin Gothic by
D R Bungay Associates, Burghfield, Berks

Printed in Great Britain by The Cromwell Press, Trowbridge, Wiltshire

CONTENTS

....

For Alex

Just starting to learn about himself and the world

ACKNOWLEDGMENTS

. . . .

George Stevens had a reputation for working slowly, but our pace on this little book makes him seem like a sprinter. One of us (Evonne) had the idea for it a decade ago, while watching a broadcast of the film and talking about the psychological issues it raises with our daughter Karon Scharpen-von Heussen. The other (Edward) was teaching Westerns at the University of Warwick. He knew that *Shane* was lacking both scholarly recognition and intelligent criticism and agreed that a book would be a great idea. Here, finally, is the result. The drafting is Edward's, but the ideas it contains stem from both of us.

British funding agencies did not look at the project with sympathy, but interviews and archive research did become possible after Edward moved to the generous and encouraging environment of Southern Methodist University in Dallas. Even with SMU's support, we still have taken our time. Remaining in England for family reasons, Evonne did a graduate degree in Health Care Policy and Management, published her research, discovered that there was no remedy under British law for victims of stalking (including our younger daughter) and worked for five years to change the situation. At the saga's end she found herself proposing legislation, advising government ministers, training police and being honoured by the Queen. In Texas, Edward wrote a much longer book (*Americans: A Collision of Histories*) as well as a great deal else, took on a book series editorship and helped to make a television series *The Story of America*. Still, we stayed with *Shane*. Thanks to the OnePass program at Continental Airlines we also stayed together.

During the time we have worked on this book we've piled up many debts of gratitude. Our greatest is to George Stevens Jr who granted us a long interview, gave us the free run of his archives on his father's work, provided introductions and generously read two drafts. Edward Buscombe first encouraged the project. Rob White welcomed our finishing it after he took over from Ed at the BFI. We missed our chance to interview Ben Johnson, and we never did get to Jack Palance or Alan Pakula, to our loss. But Ivan Moffat was most co-operative. We owe a great deal to the archivists at the Margaret Herrick Library of the Academy of Motion Picture Arts and Sciences. If former Warwick student Andy Winslow reads this, he may recognise some ideas about Ben Johnson's Chris Calloway that he developed in class.

As the manuscript took shape, Edward's SMU colleagues Ronald L. Davis, Thomas Knock and Eric Worland gave it readings and made good suggestions. So did New York film-maker Brian Breger and Iowa historian/economist Deirdre McCloskey, from the perspective of her interest in bourgeois ideology. Neil Evans and Eben Muse both offered suggestions from the far western reaches of Wales. The typescript of Ron Davis' interview with Ben Johnson for the SMU Oral History of the American Performing Arts gave us the information that Mr Johnson probably would have provided.

One summer evening in 1997, during a hot Texas weekend that Edward spent stopping, rewinding and starting the VCR, Tom Knock ran a wonderfully clear tape of *Shane* for some friends. It was great that night to sit with the dinner Tom cooked and a glass of wine and just enjoy the movie.

1

· ·

THE PUREST WESTERN OF ALL

Four brass chords sound under the Paramount 'Matterhorn' logo. Dissolve to a mountainside, in blues and greens. A horseman in buckskins enters, riding downhill. Briefly, his pistol is in centre frame. Victor Young's lilting theme music begins in strings and woodwinds and the rider stops to reconnoitre. Orange-yellow letters announce George Stevens' production of *Shane*.

Dissolve to a long shot over the valley, as the horseman crosses. Dissolve again to the valley floor in slight high angle. Under the last credits a deer can be seen in middleground, with a farmstead behind and the Grand Tetons in the distance. Cut to a child stalking the animal, cocking his gun and aiming. Cut to ground level, with the deer turning its head so that its antlers frame the approaching rider (as a tiny car crosses in the far distance). Both boy and deer see the man and each bolts. The music segues to a song sung by a woman.

Western after Western has begun with somebody coming out of the wilderness, but none uses the image with greater purity than the opening sequence of *Shane*. This film can also claim purity within the genre. Paramount advertised it that way, building on Stevens' multiple Academy Awards for previous films, on *Shane*'s Oscar nominations (including Best Director) and on the Oscar won by cinematographer Loyal Griggs. Trade and national media critics joined in celebrating *Shane*. Crowds turned out for it after its premiere on 24 April, 1953 at the Radio City Music Hall. Film-makers have been paying homage ever since. John Ford's unhappy family in *The Searchers* (1956) extrapolates themes and images that Stevens broached in *Shane* to a disillusioned, irredeemable ending. Warren Beatty and Arthur Penn drew on *Shane* in *Bonnie and Clyde* (1967). Sam Peckinpah developed the balletic violence in *The Wild Bunch* (1969) from *Shane*'s two shootings and quoted *Shane* in *Pat Garrett and Billy the Kid* (1973). Clint Eastwood remade *Shane* as *Pale Rider* (1985). Reaching beyond the Western genre, there are echoes of *Shane* in Michael Cimino's *The Deer Hunter* (1978). Mike Nichols shows *Shane*'s ending in *Primary Colors* (1998) to comment on late twentieth-century national politics ('Come back, Shane and run for President'). In *Down in the Delta* (1998) first-time film-maker Maya

Angelou reverses the shot of the child, his gun and a deer in order to make the same point about children and firearms that Stevens had intended. How shall we account for *Shane*'s power at the time of its release? How can we understand the debt to it that film-makers have felt?

George Stevens certainly knew his craft. He graduated from child actor to cameraman, shot film and wrote gags for Laurel and Hardy and directed 'Our Gang' shorts. After *Alice Adams* (1935) jumped him to first-rank features he made only twenty films, but until *The Greatest Story Ever Told* (1965), whatever Stevens released drew acclaim and made money. Seven Stevens films won Academy Awards, including Best Director twice. *Shane* and two others earned Best Director nominations and he received the Irving Thalberg Award at the Oscar ceremony in 1953. His comedies with Katharine Hepburn (*Alice Adams* and *Woman of the Year*, 1942) brought out her witty best. *Swing Time* (1936) revealed new dimensions in the dance partnership of Fred Astaire and Ginger Rogers and in the musical genre. *Gunga Din* (1939) prefigures the *Indiana Jones* cycle and thus the work of Steven Spielberg. Jean Arthur is as manic in *The More the Merrier* (1943) as she would be sober in *Shane*, her last film. From *Vivacious Lady* (1938) onward, Stevens produced his films, except for *Woman of the Year*, *I Remember Mama* (1948) and *The Only Game in Town* (1970).

Stevens was a Westerner who loved the region, but unlike Ford, Peckinpah or Eastwood he did not 'make Westerns'. *Shane* was his only one, unless we count *Annie Oakley* (1935) (which places its protagonist in Ohio with Buffalo Bill's touring show), *Gunga Din* (whose Indians wear turbans) and *Giant* (1956) (which is about family, wealth and race in modern Texas). His vaudeville childhood meant social exclusion and being an outsider was an enduring theme throughout his films. His schooling was brief and his spelling was erratic, but he read widely. He respected film studies scholars, but he always appreciated that he had helped invent their subject.

Full documentation on *Shane* survives at the Academy of Motion Picture Arts and Sciences and in such places as the Oral History of American Performing Arts Collection at Southern Methodist University and the personal records of George Stevens Jr. Using that wealth of material we can watch *Shane* develop from Jack Schaefer's novel to the final print. We can see how the film's 'intense simplicity' allows Stevens to deal with very complex themes. Finally, we can appreciate the film's influence on the Western genre. *Shane* challenges not only the historian of cultural artifacts but also the historian of cultural production.

2
....

JACK SCHAEFER, GEORGE STEVENS AND 'SHANE'

When Jack Schaefer wrote *Shane* he 'had never been west of Toledo, Ohio'. He had tried doctoral study in American literature at Columbia University and then drifted into journalism, read American history and experimented with fiction writing. *Shane* was his first result. Published in *Argosy* as a sequence of stories, it appeared as a novel in 1949. Although at first it sold poorly, its publication spurred Schaefer on to quit journalism. He kept writing about the West without seeing it. In his words, 'I had written four books about the West and still I had not been out there.' Once he and his spouse saw what he had been writing about, they moved immediately, settling in Santa Fe and remaining there until his death in 1991.

Although *Shane* deals with Anglo-whites, Schaefer explored Indian and Hispanic experience in *The Canyon* (1953) and *Old Ramon* (1956). *The Silver Whip* (Schaefer's title was *First Blood*) (1953), *Tribute to a Bad Man* (1955), *Trooper Hook* (1957) and *Advance to the Rear* (originally *Company of Cowards*) (1965) were all made into films. Schaefer's most ambitious work, *Monte Walsh* (1963), is a long cowboy elegy that became an end-of-the-West feature (William Fraker, 1970). Lee Marvin took the title role of a gentle, aging cowboy who might have been an elderly Shane. Jack Palance appeared as a figure who is even more gentle, reversing the actor's viscious persona in the Stevens film. But despite unusual subtlety, the film failed at the box office. *Shane* remains Schaefer's most famous work.

The film version is often joined with the Stevens productions *A Place in the Sun* (1951) and *Giant* in a supposed 'American trilogy'. Stevens denied any such intent, but he made the films in near sequence and each emerged from a literary attempt to make sense of America. *A Place in the Sun* is derived from Theodore Dreiser's novel *An American Tragedy*. It considers the recurrent Stevens themes of justice, ambition and success in a class-riven society and adds the issue of the state's legal violence against errant citizens. *Shane* considers violence where there is no law, both in terms of what a shooting does and as a historical problem in America's development. *Giant* adds that most intractably American question, race, which Stevens had first touched on in *Alice Adams*, through Hattie McDaniels' hired maid disrupting a middle-class dinner party. In *The Diary of Anne Frank* (1959) Stevens brought together innocence, youth, sex, racism, armed violence and the power of a malign state. Whether or not he intended an American trilogy (let alone a coherent *oeuvre*), *Shane* marks a significant point in his artistic and personal growth. Stevens' career took him from studio employment and entertainment to autonomy and arduous themes. But scholarly attention to his films consists of little more than a doctoral thesis, some short studies and a few academic articles. The only biographies are the television films made by his son George Stevens Jr, *George Stevens: A Filmmaker's Journey* (1988) and *D-Day to Berlin* (1995), which assembles the home-movie colour footage that Stevens shot for his own pleasure while he was supervising the official filming of the Allied drive across France, Belgium and Germany. This study is also short, dealing with just one film. It goes without saying that George Stevens deserves more.

3

....

INTENSE SIMPLICITY: THE STEVENS TECHNIQUE

Though his style moved from the loose fluidity of his pre-war comedies to formal composition, heroic close-ups, lingering vistas and slow dissolves, Stevens sought to bring viewers into his characters' world. In his words, 'to get some reality is the most difficult thing…about film doing. For people to create a moment of actuality.' He wanted viewers to consider a film, not receive it. 'Get 5,000 minds,' he told Robert Hughes in 1967, 'and seat them in…the Music Hall and…*calculate* the energy of these minds surpassing themselves.…I often watch the audience at work and I'm profoundly impressed by their intelligence.' In *Shane* Stevens' artifice generates an intense simplicity that hides complex meaning. The best Westerns have that quality, but most often by turning a bare bones narrative into a complex spectacle. In *The Wild Bunch* some bad men shoot up one town, wander for a time, shoot up another and die. Yet Peckinpah turned that four-statement story into one of the most intricately crafted films ever made. *Shane* presented a different problem.

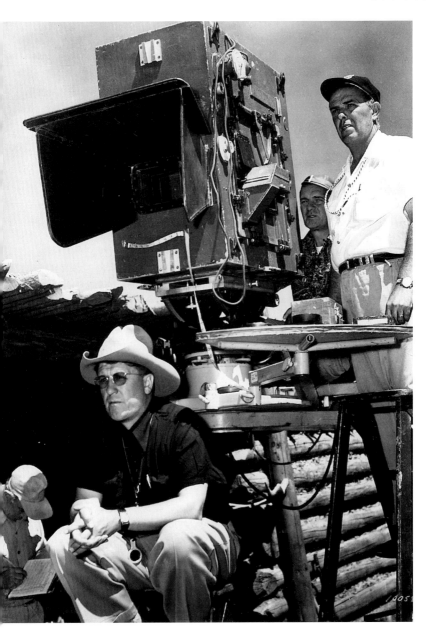

George Stevens directing on location

13

Stevens' *Shane* is true to Schaefer's purposes and the novel's possibilities, but it is not simply a 'film of the book'.

Consider the first five minutes which set in motion every issue that the film will consider: violence, American identity, social transition, family, young masculinity, being an outsider, women's place in a world that men control and choosing between incompatible desires. The voice that sings 'The Quilting Party' as the little boy races to announce that 'Somebody's coming, Pa' is slightly off-key and we see her through the open window of a cabin. She is in women's territory, though pioneer crudity surrounds her. Her husband, outside chopping a tree stump, is roughly dressed and needs a shave. Even before we learn that they are Joe Starrett (Van Heflin), Marion Starrett (Jean Arthur) and Joey Starrett (Brandon de Wilde) they carry an overtone of the Christian Holy Family.

The approaching stranger (Alan Ladd, in the title role) crosses the boundary stream without muddying its clean flow (while a few chords of his own theme replace the woman's song, in a Wagnerian leitmotif style). He avoids the garden, asks permission to cut through 'your place', and dismounts to accept some water. A close-up of the boy and a mid-shot of the woman establish the interest of each and the stranger compliments the boy's observing his approach. The child will 'make his mark'. The boy provides our point of view virtually throughout the film, but the rider's ability to watch 'things goin' on around' will drive the narrative.

When the stranger turns to take the water he reveals his holstered gun. The boy cocks his rifle, provoking a gunfighter's fast-draw. The clang of the dipper that the stranger drops breaks the idyllic quality of the soundtrack. The farmer's response is a muted challenge: 'A little touchy, aren't you?' The woman reproves the child for pointing his gun (which he has not actually done). Joey's fascination with weapons, Joe's guarded acceptance that a man will carry a gun and Marion's disapproval have all been established in the same moment. The child specifies his interest: 'I bet you can shoot.' The stranger's 'a little bit' leads to three brass chords and cowboy-style hooting, with a cut to other approaching riders. Taking Joey's rifle, the father orders the stranger to leave, which he does after requesting that the rifle be lowered. The new riders, who go through the garden, are the 'Ryker boys', named after the rancher Rufe Ryker (Emile Meyer) who employs them. Except for Rufe, his brother and foreman Morgan (John Dierkes) and cowboy Chris Calloway (Ben Johnson), 'Rykers' is all the identity they have.

Meyer gives Rufe Ryker the air of a pagan god. (Later he will use 'By Jupiter!' as an expletive.) Except in the long shot that introduces him, he doesn't wear a hat over his thick silver hair and he has a fiercely jutting beard. His accent hints of New York. He and his cowboys also carry overtones of the anti-slavery warrior John Brown, who raided against southern settlers in Kansas in 1856. He may be a rancher, but he seems somehow alien to the West. Ryker and Starrett renew an ongoing quarrel about using the land ('I've got that government beef contract and I'm gonna need all my range') and possessing it ('Now that you've told me that, will you kindly get off my place?'). They spar about descriptive nouns (Ryker: 'you and the other squatters'; Starrett: 'homesteaders, you mean') and turn to the subjects of violence ('I could blast you out of here right now'), progress ('The time for gun-blastin' a man off his own place is past') and the law ('They're building a penitentiary right now'). The Rykers mock Starrett for holding a gun. The woman comes out of the house wearing trousers. As she joins her husband and son a short right pan reveals the stranger, his pistol on prominent display. He is 'a friend of Starrett's' and his presence is enough to make the visitors withdraw. Again, they trample the garden.

The film's points of reference are now obvious. Shane's wilderness introduction and his buckskins place him among the 'Sons of Leatherstocking' as identified by cultural historian Henry Nash Smith. Like James Fenimore Cooper's literary original, these are white men who do not belong within the settled community. The woman will be tempted by him. For the little boy he will provide a dashing alternative to his stolid father. For Joe the visitor is more complex. He promises rivalry in the eyes of his wife and son. His easy courtesy conveys respect. His return in Starrett's moment of need promises protection that the farmer, his family and their kind need, but that Joe would rather not have to accept.

The arrival of the cowboys starts the familiar Western story of conflict over land and water. Settlement and private property are coming to the valley but settlement is at odds with the open-range cattleman's profit. Possessive individualism is essential to the American story of development and Joe wants to make a decent living, but *Shane* renders commerce problematic. Stevens' post-war politics were liberal, which implied a suspicion of profit-seeking. As Katharine Hepburn recalled, he cared about what film-makers did, not what they earned. In retirement, Stevens weighed his personal liking for President Lyndon Johnson against his belief that the issue in Vietnam was to do with its people not believing in private property. *Shane* specifically rejects the notion (popular among American conservatives) that the country's purpose is to enrich the individual. Getting rich is what Ryker seeks by driving the settlers out so he can meet 'that government beef contract'. As Shane and Joe point out in their shared speech during the burial sequence, all that Ryker wants is to grow his beef. The settlers want to grow their children and build a community of homes. In Ryker's world without women there can be no children, and there definitely are no homes. For all his presumed wealth, Ryker sleeps in a room above Grafton's bar.

Stevens crafted the film's simple opening out of difficult materials. These included the original novel, A. B. Guthrie Jr's first draft of the script, the advice of co-workers, including historical consultant Joe De Yong, and the director's own habit of shooting vastly more film than would ever appear in the final cut. Schaefer's introductory paragraphs to his novel are almost as classically elegant as Stevens' first shots:

> He rode into our valley in the summer of '89. I was a kid then, barely topping the backboard of father's old chuck-wagon. I was on the upper rail of our small corral, soaking in the late afternoon sun, when I saw him far down the road, where it swung into the valley from the open plains beyond.
>
> In that clear Wyoming air I could see him plainly, though he was still several miles away. There seemed nothing remarkable about him, just another stray horseman riding up the road toward the cluster of frame buildings that was our town. Then I saw a pair of cowhands, loping past him, stop and stare after him with curious intentness.
>
> He came steadily on, straight through the town without slackening pace, until he reached the fork a half-mile below our place. One branch turned left across the river ford and on to Luke Fletcher's big spread. The other bore ahead along the right bank where we homesteaders had pegged our claims in a row up the valley. He hesitated briefly, studying the choice and moved again steadily on our side.
>
> As he came near, what impressed me most was his clothes. He wore dark trousers of some serge material tucked into tall boots and held at the waist by a wide belt, both of a soft black leather tooled in

intricate design. A coat of the same dark material as the trousers was neatly folded and strapped to his saddle-roll. His shirt was finespun linen, rich brown in color. The handkerchief knotted loosely around his throat was black silk. His hat was not the familiar Stetson, not the familiar gray or muddy tan. It was plain black, soft in texture, unlike any I had ever seen, with a creased crown and a wide curling brim, swept down in front to shield the face.

One change is obvious, identifying Shane with Nature rather than with the bad man, town-centred tradition betokened by a dark, faded-elegant costume. Renaming the cattleman also bears weight. Fletcher (an arrowmaker) connotes both danger and the West's Indian past. But Stevens had seen the consequences of Nazism and Ryker (Reicher) might well have conveyed a malign desire for power.

Another change is the time setting. Schaefer places the story in 1889, one year before the Census Bureau announced that the 'frontier' had ended. He has his narrator telling the story in about 1893. Stevens changed the film's setting from 1889 to an indeterminate nineteenth-century 'West-time'. That let him make an important historical reference to the Civil War (1861–5) as having been in the near past. Abandoning flashback and specific dating also freed him from showing a more developed valley in the never filmed framing sequences. One proposal was to use a railroad sign to identify the town as 'Shane, Wyoming'. *The Man Who Shot Liberty Valance* (John Ford, 1961) uses the railroad very effectively to ask what price in vitality was paid for progress. *Shane* is about progress, but including railroads and a latter-day town name would have overburdened the film.

In his old age Stevens speculated that the story had overtones of medieval knighthood. He toyed with weaving the story together with 'Jack the Giant Killer' being told by the mother to the son. The first draft of the script closes with her telling the child that 'all the giants are dead' and him responding, 'I know what you mean, Mother. Shane and us got the best of all the giants, even the biggest one.' None of this was used. The medieval theme receives the barest allusion with the heraldic chords that greet the Paramount logo at the beginning and with the sense that the man in buckskin is errant, if not a knight. The boy does listen to a story, but it is never specified as 'Jack'. We still can understand the film as a fairy tale with Shane disappearing at the end into his 'never-never-world, whatever that might be', a point Stevens made during a public lecture at Ohio State University in 1973. *Shane* is about a child's experience of the world's complexity, which fairy tales interpret. But the film is also about adult responsibilities. As Stevens noted during shooting, 'Shane should be going somewhere when this story starts and the whole piece must be a temporary interruption of this.'

The child figure changes in the crossover from book to film. Schaefer's Bob is a half-grown schoolboy who has trouble with the teacher, wins playground fights and skips school to go fishing. Stevens' Joey is a *little* boy. Somewhat androgynous, he is almost without other children's company. He would never fight or sneak off from school and he is driven to confess when he sneaks a look at Shane's pistol.

Also transformed in Stevens' version is the element of commerce. Schaefer's Starretts live in a white clapboard house, not a cabin. Its next improvement will be a parlour, the nineteenth century's symbol of gentility. In the novel Shane establishes himself with the family by saving Starrett from a price-gouging peddler who has brought a new cultivator from Cheyenne. He begins to win the woman's heart because he can talk ribbons and bonnets with her. That strikes both father and son as strange, but does not unman him; it merely places him beyond their range. The novel's town has several stores and a school. The film's town has just three businesses: a hotel, a general store plus bar, and a blacksmith shop. Every point the novel develops receives its moment in the film, except for Shane's knowledge of fashion. But reducing much of what Schaefer wrote to the barest minimum gave Stevens space for the problems of identity and of public and private morality that really concerned him and that give the film its continuing power.

4

. . . .

STEVENS' 'SHANE': A SYNOPSIS

The remainder of the narrative is simple. The family welcomes Shane. He savours their domesticity and accepts a job. He attacks the stump Joe had been chopping and the two men defeat it (with rapid cross-cutting as they swing their axes). They are bonding on Joe's ground, literally. Joe sends Shane to town for barbed wire and work clothes, markers of the old West's replacement by what the Starretts represent.

Though Joey 'is too young to go loaded', the boy wants bullets for his gun. He play-shoots 'Rykers' and asks his father for a shooting lesson. Settler Ernie Wright (Leonard Strong) arrives on a buckboard, the sign of either womanhood or ineffectual masculinity. He has had enough harassment from 'them Ryker boys' and is 'pulling stakes'. His quarrel seems to be with Starrett, rather than with the cowboys who have cut his fences and driven their steers through his wheat. Starrett persuades him to stay for 'one last hand' and calls a meeting of the settlers.

Shane's arrival in town is watched by the family of settler Fred Lewis (Edgar Buchanan) and by storekeeper/innkeeper Grafton (Paul McVey). A cowboy whom we will learn is Chris Calloway comes through the half-doors between the bar (where men drink) and the store (a place for the settlers and their women). He leers at Lewis' daughter Susan (Janice Carroll) as she preens with a new hat. In a subplot that was filmed but eliminated during editing, his leer turns into flirtation and then into courtship as he escapes from the cowboys' sterile world. Shane changes into denim clothes, enters the bar to get Joey a soda pop and declines Chris' challenge to fight, which Lewis observes from the store. The settlers meet that evening to make plans. They scorn Shane for cowardice and he withdraws from the meeting.

The settlers go to town together, which amuses the cowboys. Shane, still in denim, takes Joey's empty soda bottle into the bar. Chris once again challenges him and Shane wins the fight. Ryker offers him employment and suggests that Marion is the reason why Shane refuses his offer. The cowboys attack Shane while the farmers stand by. Joe joins the fray and the two men stand off their enemies, bonding now on Shane's ground. The sequence

Shane and Joe defeat the stump

closes with Ryker sending a messenger to Cheyenne and promising gunsmoke at the next confrontation. Meanwhile, back at the farm, Marion tends the men's wounds and Joey tells his mother that he 'just loves Shane'.

The next sequence opens with the arrival of another stranger (Walter Jack Palance), walking his horse along the valley floor to a soundtrack of heavy chords in deep brass and percussion. He wears a black hat and two guns, but the rest of his costume is white and brown. He enters the saloon as a dog slinks out, orders coffee rather than the conventional whisky and announces that Ryker has sent for him. At the farm Marion tries on different dresses, finally settling on her wedding gown. Shane gives Joey the shooting lesson that his father keeps postponing. Marion reproves him, saying that she doesn't want guns in the valley, including Shane's. The family goes to join the other settlers and celebrate Independence Day.

The cowboys also celebrate with a raucous rodeo. The Stranger and the Ryker brothers are in the saloon when the Southern settler Stonewall Torrey (Elisha Cook Jr) enters, gathering bluster with a few drinks. When he stomps out he breaks the louvres of the door. We see the gunman's leering face through the gap. A dissolve transforms the broken louvres into the stripes of the American flag and a crane shot up and back presents the settler celebration with dancing and simple fireworks. The day is also Joe and Marion's wedding anniversary, which we learn after the women of the group pull the men away from the bottle that Torrey has brought. Torrey tells the other men about the new stranger and Shane identifies him as 'a man named Wilson', to some settlers' disquiet about Shane himself. When the dancing resumes, Marion dances with Shane.

The Starretts and Shane return by night to the farm where the Rykers are waiting. Ryker offers to buy Starrett out and give both him and Shane top-pay employment. Starrett refuses and they resume their debate, framing it around both the historical question of the valley's past and the future problem of its development. Wilson and Shane silently eye each other while Joey watches. The uninvited visitors depart, obeying Starrett's command that they keep out of the garden.

The fearful but sensible Swedish settler Shipstead (Douglas Spencer) and Torrey ride together into town. The Swede needs blacksmith work and the Southerner will protect him and get a drink. Wilson goads Torrey into losing his temper; he pulls his revolver and Wilson shoots him in 'self-defence'. The Swede takes the body away. The intent is to provoke Starrett into a thoughtless reaction, which nearly happens. Lewis decides to leave but Starrett holds the settlers together so that Torrey can have the burial his bravery has earned.

The burial takes place on a hilltop looking down towards the town, while the Ryker men watch from the saloon porch. Cross-cutting between the funeral and the town, the camera lingers on Chris Calloway. As the funeral breaks up, Ryker's men set fire to Lewis' abandoned homestead. Starrett and Shane rally the settlers. Lewis changes his mind about leaving and the community returns to the farm to put out the fire. At this point Ryker realises that Starrett is holding the group together.

At the Starrett homestead a 'peace party' invites Joe to parley on the premise that 'things have gone too far' and that Ryker is a 'reasonable man'. Starrett determines to go, buckling on his revolver and arguing with Marion, while Joey plays with a wooden pistol. Shane goes out to the Starrett barn and Chris arrives to tell him that he is leaving Ryker and that Joe is 'up against a stacked deck'. Clad again in buckskin and wearing his pistol, Shane returns to the house and tells Starrett that this is his, Shane's, game. He defeats Joe in a brawl. Shane and Marion bid farewell with a handshake. Shane rides to town and Joey follows on foot.

Shane confronts Ryker in the saloon, telling him that both their times are over. He kills both Wilson and Ryker. Joey, who has been watching from beneath the door, sees Morgan taking aim with a rifle from the upper level. He warns Shane who kills Morgan but is wounded by Morgan's shot. Shane says goodbye to Joey and rides away despite the boy's fervent pleading to come back. In the penultimate shot Shane is ascending the same mountainside that he rode down in the opening credit sequence. The final shot shows him still climbing a hill, away from the point of view. But he slumps in the saddle and he is passing through the tombstones of the little town's graveyard which, we know, lies far below the mountains.

5

. . . .

THE PRODUCTION OF 'SHANE'

Giving 1952 as the year of *Shane*'s production is mere convenience. Paramount bought the rights to the novel in 1949 and offered it to Stevens on 1 June, 1950 'as an Alan Ladd vehicle'. George Stevens Jr remembers that he was 'working during the summer for my father reading material ... [including] *Shane* and ... talking with him in his bedroom about it'. Stevens requested reviews of the book and found there were hardly any. Nobody could have predicted then that *Shane* would eventually appear in a university press critical edition.

Stevens accepted on 'the assumption that regardless of [Paramount's] omissions in the past you will from now on perform all of the terms and conditions of the contract'. He told his associate Fred Guiol that he wanted to start 'as soon as possible', though he was deeply involved with *A Place in the Sun* and had *Something to Live For* in preparation. He continued to bristle towards Paramount whose 'refusal to fix ... dates [for production] ... and ... evasion of ... responsibilities ... show most clearly your abuse in the management of this contract'.

The search for a scriptwriter took almost six months and no thought was given to Schaefer. Seventeen names were submitted to Stevens, including the studio's initial suggestion of W. R. Burnett, Richard Llewellyn (*How Green Was My Valley*), William Saroyan (who had been a member of the Stevens team in Europe) and Christopher Isherwood (in what Ivan Moffat called 'an off-beat suggestion because he's a sensitive, human writer with a world-wide reputation, though not for being a dramatist'). Among the nominees was Jack Sher, who did receive credit for additional dialogue. Only three – Sydney Boehm, Harry Brown and Charles Marquis Warren – had associations with the Western genre.

Stevens himself looked beyond Hollywood and decided on novelist/professor A. B. Guthrie Jr who had won the Pulitzer Prize for *The Big Sky*. Just as Schaefer did not work on *Shane* the film, Guthrie did not write the script for Howard Hawks' production of his own book which, George Stevens Jr recalls, 'was filming in the next valley'. Guthrie was 'not enthusiastic' about leaving his classes at the University of Kentucky. Direct persuasion by Stevens and an offer of $1,500 per week for four weeks' work and then week-by-week pay until the script was finished changed his mind. On 11 January, 1951 he signed on.

Guthrie proved skilful and swift. Within a weekend he produced twenty pages of dialogue. He did possess two guides to what Stevens wanted: one was the Schaefer novel; the other, almost certainly, was Stevens' careful annotation of the book. Though Stevens' marginal notes are undated, we can assume that he made them before Guthrie's draft and that Guthrie saw them, because many points that Stevens noted turn up in Guthrie's script. In effect, the notes present the first draft which Guthrie then turned into a worked-up script.

A fair amount of dialogue in the film was taken straight from the book, and Stevens rather than Guthrie chose it. The choices range from the simple ('call me Shane') to extended speeches such as Joe's wordy explanation to Shane about why small farm beef production is an improvement on open range ranching. Stevens also noted points to transform. Schaefer gives Starrett a small speech warning his son not to get attached to the visitor; he is 'fiddle-footed' and will be moving on. It is just a sensible caution to a naive child. In the film, the warning comes from Marion, who tells Joey not to 'get to liking Shane too much', because she 'doesn't want [him] to'. She is warning herself against temptation as much as cautioning the boy. The change also helps establish Joey as his mother's naive surrogate, saying what she cannot.

Stevens filled the margins of the novel with comments like 'curtain', 'climax', 'good scene' and 'use this scene'. He even began planning shots. Next to Schaefer's description of the bar-room fight he wrote: 'make Chris face up between cuts he goes behind the table and comes up with a bloody

face'. When the ranch men's pressure on the farmers begins to tell, Stevens turned a long speech by Joe into 'show all of this in shots'. He saw the dramatic possibilities in the ranchers' second encounter with Starrett, which became the night-time debate at the homestead. He told himself to 'get this tenseness in the picture', 'use the best thing in the picture', 'wait this out with big c.u.s. [close ups] back and forth', and finally, 'this is the gimmick' that will propel the film into its final resolution. Stevens had learned to write for the camera in his 'Our Gang' and Laurel and Hardy days. *Shane* shows him writing for the scriptwriter and thinking from the start about how to turn literature into cinema.

After Stevens' death, actor after actor praised his willingness to listen to ideas. They also told of how he coped with studio interference by listening, seeming to agree and then doing what he had already planned. He wasted no energy on arguments. His handling of Guthrie is a case in point. When Stevens talked about making *Shane* he credited Guthrie for a script very close to what was finally released. In fact, it is not. Had what he written been filmed, it would have been a 'film of the book', transliterated from narrative prose into dialogue, but not translated from novel into cinema. Achieving such a translation only began with what Stevens wrote.

Stevens' aim was simplification of the script. Confronted with one particularly banal line ('Johnson's coming after all'), Stevens scrawled 'this line just won't do'. When the farmers are planning their response to the Ryker harassment the script has one farmer saying 'that's all, I guess and if it don't amount to much, still it's better 'n no scheme at all'. The director's note is 'this kind of talk just won't go'. It was Stevens' idea to have Shane change into denim clothes before the first meeting with Chris, transforming the cowboy's bar room bravado towards a newcomer into a confrontation between ways of life.

Consider how we meet the minor characters. Historical consultant Joe De Yong proposed a speech for Fred Lewis at the farmers' meeting: 'Reckin I ain't been cut out to be much of a hee-ro. Got th' notion pretty well fixed in mind a long time ago that the best I could expect outa life was t' break even. But I ain't enny ball-uh-fire at bettin' on even that much.' Stevens' introduction of Lewis in Grafton's store, when Shane first comes in to get wire for Starrett and work clothes for himself, is much more effective. Overweight and nondescript, Lewis is shown lounging while his wife and daughters shop. The bartender brings him a flask, slipping it to him so that the women don't see. Shane's request for soda pop (for Joey)

prompts the store-keeper's wish that 'more men around here would drink it', thinking of Lewis rather than of the cowboys beyond the swinging doors. Lewis sees Shane's refusal to accept Chris' challenge as he peeps into the bar room where he does not dare go himself. He is the source of Shane being scorned as a coward at the farmers' meeting. When Shane shows his mettle in the second fight, Lewis shows his too, cowering

Torrey at the settler picnic

outside with the line, 'This isn't good'. Stevens shows that Lewis is no 'ball-uh-fire' cinematically without the need for speeches or descriptions.

The only introduction during the meeting that really counts is Elisha Cook Jr's Southern bantam, Stonewall Torrey. His arrival provokes a burst of 'Marching Through Georgia' from a minor character playing a harmonica. His belligerent first line, 'That's enough out of you, Yank', invokes conventional imagery of the defiant South. 'Yank' and the 'Reb' being in the same place invokes the equally conventional image of the West as a place where the wounds of the Civil War could heal. Cook's small-time loser persona combines with his bluster here to prepare us for his inevitable death. As scripted, the meeting was a wooden, character-by-character introduction. As filmed, it reveals complexities and helps drive both the film's moral development and its story line.

Guthrie's full script was completed by April 1951. Stevens' marginal notes on the draft were made before location shooting began in Wyoming. The notes establish his primary strategies of driving towards narrative simplicity and of using cinematic means rather than words to make his points. They show the direction in which further refinement would go during shooting itself, as partial drafts emerged during story conferences and from on-set collaborators. Some important changes did not happen until filming was underway. The rancher is renamed Ryker; Bob Starrett becomes Joey; Torrey is made a former Confederate and given the nickname Stonewall, whereas in the novel he is a mere settler. Shane gets the chance to state his position about weapons ('a gun is only a tool, Marion') after hearing Marion's wish that there should be no guns in the valley when she interrupts the shooting lesson with Joey. Where the notes are in Stevens' handwriting (and with his inimitable spelling, such as 'Gene' Arthur or a shot from this 'angel'), the idea tended to make its way into the film. Where the effect would have been to add complication and wordiness, the idea did not.

That the Stevens technique of writing for the camera, shooting an enormous amount of footage and then editing down was different from how John Ford or Alfred Hitchcock worked is no news. Yet Stevens was as in control as either Ford or Hitchcock. Stevens was a master improviser, a technique which he learned working with Laurel and Hardy and on the 'Our Gang' comedies. He improvised with spectacular success when he confected *Gunga Din* from the Kipling poem, the personas of Douglas Fairbanks Jr, Cary Grant, Sam Jaffe and Victor

McLaglen and the enormous army camp and battle sequences that required endless shooting. Stevens also had a rare talent for turning books into cinematically realised films. The first was *Alice Adams*, derived from a Booth Tarkington novel. He refined his skill on *Quality Street*, *I Remember Mama* and, most recently before *Shane*, *A Place in the Sun*. *Shane* reflects both aspects of his artistic development: rapid on-the-edge improvisation and an ability to adapt large-scale literary texts. But it is much more the product of knowing where he wanted to take the film before he started shooting than of simply making it up as he went along.

Though Paramount saw *Shane* as 'an Alan Ladd vehicle', Stevens' first choice for Shane was Montgomery Clift, as a note shows on the novel ('monty must train to show mussels [sic] for tree chopping'). Ladd at first doubted the project, and, according to Joel McCrea, it was he, McCrea, who convinced him to take the role. The widely publicised initial choice for Starrett was William Holden, who expressed interest but dropped out after a small war of press releases in the trade papers. Van Heflin, who replaced him, brought considerable stage experience, a factor that worked to his advantage given that his character has more speeches than any other and has to deal with complex emotions. There was little doubt that Jean Arthur would play Marion, despite her being better known for comedies. Brandon de Wilde ('the best child actor available', in George Stevens Jr's words) was the only choice for the boy, despite stage commitments that took him away during shooting.

The choice of Ben Johnson for Chris Calloway marked a break in the actor's career. He had already made four films for John Ford in roles that were 'taciturn, good-humoured and dignified', as well as having minor parts in three other productions. Years later Johnson told the film historian Ronald L. Davis that until *Shane*, all he really did was play himself. In the low-budget (but deeply felt) *Wagonmaster* (1950) Ford had given Johnson the chance to break through as an action star. *Shane*, however, marks Johnson's first role with any psychological complexity, pointing towards his powerful Tector Gorch in *The Wild Bunch* and his Oscar-winning post-Western role in *The Last Picture Show* (Peter Bogdanovich, 1971).

From the beginning, Stevens planned to shoot much of the film in Wyoming. He found a spectacular and virtually untouched location at Jackson Hole, working on land owned by the Rockefeller Foundation, north of the hamlet of Kelly. How he used the location demonstrates

Stevens' careful, deceptive artifice. The set appears to be watered country, with the Grand Tetons not far away. In fact, the site is dry sagebrush plain, the stream that flows by the Starrett homestead was artificial and the mountains are much farther away than they appear. Stevens achieved their looming effect by foreshortening with a strong telephoto lens. George Stevens Jr recalls how he:

> went with him on his initial location scout and . . . how we would end up somewhere in a car and he would walk and walk and walk in the shadow of the Teton Mountains until he found the exact spot of where to plant the trees on the hill that would mark the entrance toward the town and how the town was going to relate to the cemetery on the other hill above. This is one of the aspects of a cinematic mind that is seldom explored. He was intent on finding a way to juxtapose the landscape and the sets so the audience would have vivid visual reference points.

Only a few location sets were needed: the town, the Starrett homestead, the cemetery and three other settler cabins. An interior set of the Starrett cabin was built in the gymnasium of Jackson Hole High School in case of inclement weather. It was a wise precaution.

Location shooting began on 25 July, 1951. Encouraging his own version of method acting, Stevens wore Western costume (as he often did anyway) and had Western music (not Victor Young's score) played between takes. The unstable Wyoming weather began to plague the production immediately. Even on the first day work was delayed until late afternoon because of clouds and showers. There was another delay on 26 July when the bad weather forced a retreat to the gymnasium for interior work, restricting shooting to close-ups. Between the start of principal photography and the end of first-unit location work on 4 September there were thirty-one days of shooting and twenty-six were disturbed by the weather. By 4 August production was a full day behind because of weather delays. *Shane* was twenty-seven days behind schedule when filming ended on 19 October.

Stevens took what advantage he could of the weather, telling cameraman Loyal Griggs to keep shooting despite cloudy skies and thunderstorms. (There were precedents, most notably John Ford's use of a spectacular desert thunderstorm in *She Wore a Yellow Ribbon* (1949), but this wouldn't have mattered given Stevens' independence from the work of others.) The clouds and thunderstorm play to strong effect at the moment of Torrey's killing by Wilson. The recurrent cloudiness during the location shooting makes plausible the decision to drench Shane with studio rain when he leaves the farmers' meeting at the Starrett homestead.

Yet when Stevens wanted bad weather he could not get it. He intended to film Torrey's funeral in overcast weather but shot most of it on 17 August, the only full day of clear light during the entire outdoor production (on a location that turned out to be a giant anthill, to the actors' great discomfort). The good light allowed Stevens to take a drawn-out panning shot of the entire funeral party, which transformed itself without a cut into an extreme long-shot of the town, with the cattlemen on the porch of Grafton's saloon and the empty land and mountains beyond. This single shot makes several statements: about the grief that accompanies the end of a life, about guilt and callousness, and about the tininess of individual experience within the greater framework of the world. That it all takes place under a smiling, warm sun rather than amid conventional gloom only adds to the strength of the points that are being made.

The weather was not the only reason production fell behind. On the first day of filming Stevens managed to get eighteen takes with nine set-ups, despite not being able to start until late afternoon. He was working with enormous 'blimped' Technicolor cameras that ran three strips of film at once, making them time consuming to reload as well as cumbersome to move. On 26 July there were twenty takes with seventeen set-ups. Two days later there were no fewer than fifty-six takes on nineteen set-ups. When Stevens wanted to work fast, he could, but as the amount of film in the can began to grow, he began spending longer and longer getting just one shot. On 3 August he made five takes of Joey entering the Starrett homestead and the following day eight takes of a close-up of Starrett at the dinner table. Stevens' son was company clerk on the production, with responsibility for listing the takes. He recalls the seven takes it took to get the arrival of Ernie Wright at the Starrett farm to announce he is departing: 'It was such a cinematic way to handle a scene of exposition. The Tetons with the perfect clouds in the background, the father and son talking as the boy jumps on and off the log while the figure in the horse-drawn cart approaches in the distance. Two things going on at once.' But it took a lot of shooting.

Stevens shot major sequences as single pieces when he could. The entire shooting lesson between Shane and Joey was filmed over two days, 10–11 August, with seventy-two takes on the first day of work and forty-seven on the second. On the first day there were twenty-nine set-ups, requiring two hours and forty-four minutes of set-up time, two hours of rehearsal time and two hours forty-five minutes of shooting time. On the second day there were sixteen set-ups, two hours forty-three minutes of set-up time, one hour and twenty-two minutes of rehearsal time and an hour and fourteen minutes of shooting time. Stevens needed eight takes of Joey asking Shane to teach him to shoot, eleven of Shane showing Joey how to shoot, twelve of Shane shooting and five of Marion's condemnation of the whole business. Fifteen takes were needed to get Shane shooting the rock that Joey has asked him to hit, and six to get Joey's reaction. Years later Jean Arthur recalled her amazement both at Stevens' patience as he directed the little boy and at de Wilde's ability to keep doing what he was asked. It was by taking such great care that Stevens got the material he could edit down. But it was very expensive. 'Slow progress' appears often in the reasons why location production fell behind. Slow progress caused the studio delays. That was how Stevens worked.

When the crew returned to Hollywood there was still a great deal of work to do. All the interiors in Grafton's store remained to be shot, including Shane's first scene with Chris, their fight, Torrey's bar-room blustering that sets him up to be killed, and Shane's final confrontation with Ryker and Wilson. So did the 'outdoor' Fourth of July sequence, which took four days of work with a specialist dance coach and company, and the battle between Starrett and Shane over who would go to town to face Ryker and his hired killer. When shooting finally ended on 19 October, the total amount of good footage was 363,102 feet; the film's final release length was 10,600 feet.

Only skimpy information survives about post-production, which extended through much of 1952. Credit for editing went to William Hornbeck and Tom McAdoo, but Stevens did most of the editing himself. According to his son, he did not use a cutting room. Instead he set up a small screening room with about fifteen chairs with control switches for the two projectors on either side of his chair. This enabled him to run the projected image backwards and forwards on a large screen. He would look at the edited scene on one projector and then switch to the other machine to run alternative takes that he was considering.

Only a handful of notes survive from the process. McAdoo thought of presenting 'Joey's face behind bush' as he is introduced stalking the deer just after the credits. From the few notes in his own handwriting, Stevens' direction remained clear, simplifying as far as he could while intensifying the emotional and dramatic points that he wanted to make. After the first preview, which took place 7 July, 1952, studio associate Charles West suggested one major cut, dropping the 'Jack the Giant Killer' material and urging that 'the Fourth of July Party might be shortened to advantage'. Jack Sher (responsible for additional dialogue) proposed that Chris Calloway's moral redemption and warning to Shane about the final meeting between Starrett and Ryker be cut, on the grounds that 'it doesn't seem believable. ... A gunman like Shane ... would know ... Starrett knows too ... so Chris riding up is completely unnecessary.' Unlike the 'Giant Killer' material it did further the narrative, in that it provided Shane with a positive reason to resume his former persona and intervene on Joe's behalf. So it stayed.

Shane was produced during one of American society's binges of public prudery. Schaefer salted his novel with what at the time passed for strong language, meaning eighteen mentions of 'hell' or 'damn', one of them a 'God-damned'. In 1954 Houghton Mifflin published a 'school edition' in which the swearing was changed so as not to offend 'secondary school boards and librarians'. The film production faced the same problem. Consider the question of why Shane stays with Starrett, which is first raised explicitly after he defeats Chris in their bar-room fight. As realised, Ryker responds to Shane's refusal to join him at first with straightforward puzzlement. Then, filling the screen, he leers 'pretty wife Starrett's got'. Shane replies, 'why you dirty slinkin' old man'. Guthrie's original dialogue was 'for an old timer, you're a measly man'. Stevens' own choice was 'son of a bitch'. But that was not acceptable.

The Production Code administration wanted only a few cuts which Stevens for the most part resisted. The one proposed cut that would have counted was the manner of Torrey's killing, which was far more important to the film's purposes than any 'hells', 'damns', or 'sons of bitches'. Had it gone, much of what the director intended would have been lost. The killing stayed as Stevens shot and edited it, making a small chink in the Production Code's power and marking a significant break in how Hollywood films deal with the very American issue of deadly violence.

6
....

STEVENS AND AMERICAN HISTORY: MATTERS OF FACT

All Westerns are about history. For some, history is a vague past that provides handy symbols and conventions. Others attempt what an academic historian might try to achieve, reconsidering a major figure or event in the light of fresh knowledge and of latter-day sensibilities. Still other films use outright fiction for the sake of a symbolic meditation on what the American people are, how they became that way and whether or not they ought to be pleased with themselves.

The whole genre is only one element in a discourse that began when Europeans first imposed their own willing selves and very unwilling Africans on the landscape and its native people. That discourse has gone on in poetry, written fiction, drama, the plastic arts, dance, music and academic and popular history. Before there was a United States, the literate offspring of Protestant England made their poetry of God's high purposes in the New World, their narratives of Indian captivity, their formal historiography and their secular history paintings a huge device for imposing their own meanings upon a process that involved many others. Very few peoples have argued more incessantly than have the Americans about the process and the meaning of their own existence. The American West has provided one of the most recurrent themes in that argument.

When the British film critic Philip French considered Clint Eastwood's *Shane* remake, *Pale Rider*, he noted that for roughly forty years after 1939 Western movies offered a potent means for carrying on this very American debate. Some would say that Eastwood's *The Outlaw Josey Wales* (1976), which collapses virtually all historical referents into the bleak assertion that everybody involved had lost something in 'that damn [Civil] war', marked the effective end of that cycle. Though *Josey Wales* bears little direct reference to *Shane*, Eastwood's Southern dirt farmer title character belongs to a line of descent that includes Stonewall Torrey. If *Stagecoach* marked the onset of the Western's great cycle and *Josey Wales* marked its conclusion, *Shane*'s release in 1953 came at the cycle's mid-point, not strictly in chronological terms, but rather in terms of the genre's development. Stevens' film presents a significant statement in the intellectual history of American society within an epoch that began with the onset of the Second World War, crested with victory over Japan and the

Fascist powers, found new complexities about itself during the Korean War, and ended with the bitter, self-recriminating aftermath of the Vietnam War.

Shane offers history in the guise of a meditation about symbol and myth, rather than by reconstructing an event like the Sioux/Cheyenne/Arapaho victory over Custer at Little Big Horn. There are no Indians in *Shane*, although Ryker has a Cheyenne arrowhead in his shoulder. Custer is probably dead and Tashunca-uitco (Crazy Horse) and Ta tan `ka I-yo-ta'-ke (Sitting Bull) pose no danger. The farmers, the Rykers, Grafton, Shane, Wilson are all entirely fictitious characters, with any resemblance to living or dead historical persons being (as the saying goes) purely coincidental.

The snow-capped Grand Tetons tell us that the setting is not Texas or Arizona, as does the absence of Hispanics. The only explicit mention of where the story is set is a barely audible 'Wyoming', after Torrey asks the bar-room drinkers to drink a Fourth of July toast to 'the greatest state in the union'. The Southerner's own answer is 'the sovereign state of Alabama'. A viewer who has any knowledge of Wyoming history will recognise that the actual historical point of reference is the Johnson County Range War, which culminated with an orgy of violence by ranchers against supposed cattle rustlers in 1892. When Michael Cimino returned to this theme in *Heaven's Gate* (1980) he made that reference unambiguous.

That Stevens did not do so does not mean that he was uninterested in American history. On the contrary, historical accuracy was central to his purpose. He sought verisimilitude in the film's settings and costumes and in situations that could have existed in the time and the place of the story. He wanted to impart the grittiness of Western life. In late-life interviews he explained that he was attacking the image of singing-cowboy glamour (which, in fact, reached backwards from Roy Rogers and Gene Autry to Tom Mix and to 'Buffalo Bill's Wild West and Congress of Rough Riders of the World'). He had dealt with that theme long before in *Annie Oakley*. In *Shane* he was joining a non-glamorous tradition of Westerns that included Howard Hawks' *Red River* (1947), John Ford's *My Darling Clementine* (1946) and *Drums Along the Mohawk* (1939), the silent films of William S. Hart, as well as the art of Frederic Remington, Charles Schreyvogel and Charles M. Russell. He did study Remington's and Russell's paintings, but his son and biographer George Stevens Jr doubts whether he ever saw *Clementine* or *Drums*. The parallel between his visual aesthetic and what Hawks and Ford presented is not a sign that he was being derivative of these directors; it is one instance of the frequent pattern of an idea being 'in the air' and of different cultural producers seizing upon it.

Stevens commissioned extensive research in photographic archives and nineteenth-century engravings, particularly from the pages of *Harper's Magazine*. He wanted images of celebrations and group picnics, particularly those held on the Fourth of July. He used an anvil and gunpowder for the Independence Day fireworks because research showed that is what the farmers would have used. Before he dropped Joe's encounter with a peddler about a cultivator, he wanted to know whether it would have been a Studebaker or a McCormick. Changing the Starrett house from white clapboards to bare timbers suited homesteaders who had not been long on the land. Showing the town as just a few buildings was true to how towns of that time often looked. As Stevens put it, 'the only reason that there were two sides of the street in Western movies was because if they didn't have another side of the street you'd see Culver City'.

Stevens paid great attention to the costumes on the film. He asked assistants to 'check women's fashions 1889' and insisted that the costumes should not look as if they came from the Paramount wardrobe department or from the Western Costume Company. The director vetoed Van Heflin's wish to wear an expensive shirt from Abercrombie and Fitch as part of Joe's costume. Instead, all the farmers wore plain, hard-worn gear in earthen tones. The goal was akin to what he had achieved in *A Place in the Sun* when he costumed Shelley Winters' factory girl from a used-clothes store, dramatising the contrast between her and the rich young woman played by Elizabeth Taylor. Stevens wanted his settlers to look like they had endured the hard, grinding work and the frustration of carving farmsteads upon the valley floor.

To improve the authenticity of the production, the redoubtable Joe De Yong was hired as technical adviser. De Yong was hearing-impaired and preferred to communicate in writing. He issued long memos on matters ranging from how Wyoming farmers piled their firewood (standing it on end, rather than lying it flat, as de Yong noticed in Jackson Hole) to sketches of the past lives of the characters. He told Stevens what a roving man like Shane would do when he stopped for water (care for the horse first, loosening the saddle and bridle so the animal could drink). He suggested that if the farmstead bordered on a swift-flowing stream (as the

Starrett place does), the owner would not bother with a water trough for the livestock. He had ideas about how a frontierswoman might conduct herself in a moment of tension, based on having seen Tom Mix's wife confront the drunken star with a butcher knife beneath her apron. He wrote very wordy dialogue which Stevens hardly used, except for one memorable line given to Ernie Wright about the futility of meetings, where men did nothing but 'poke holes in the air with their fingers'.

Taken by itself, such close attention to historical detail might have ended up providing no more than antiquarian accuracy, not historical believability. However, Stevens knew when not to worry about detail. One instance is Marion's first appearance, wearing trousers. Even on an isolated farmstead, a woman of her time would hardly ever have violated the conventions of gender presentation, unless she consciously intended to cross-dress (something which did happen, but it was as risky then as male crossdressing is now). The greater convenience of trousers for farm work (or even for crossing the plains with a wagon train) made no difference. As we will see, the choice of Marion's quasi-male initial costume is made for other reasons. The historical research that Stevens commissioned served the production rather than dominated it.

7
. . . .
STEVENS AND HISTORY: HOW CHANGE HAPPENS

A more difficult historical issue reaches beyond specific fact. This is how to trace the transition between one historical situation, one way of understanding and organising the world and another. A viewer with any sophistication about American history will recognise the moment when *Shane* becomes explicitly didactic. This is the moonlight debate on the farmstead, as Ryker and Starrett argue out their differences about the past and the future. In this scene they repeat the argument about 'The Significance of the Frontier in American History' that historian Frederick Jackson Turner presented to the American Historical Association in Chicago in 1893. Let us look at what Turner wrote, at its influence, at how it made its way into *Shane*, and at how the film used this piece of academic writing for its own purposes.

Writing in a more poetic style than a pedantic one, Turner set out to make sweeping sense of American history. His central propositions were simple. First, Americans were what they were because for centuries they had enjoyed free land. Compared to the drama of taking up that land, dividing it and using it, all other questions faded, even the conflict between the free-labour North and the slave regime in the South. Second, Americans had stripped themselves free of previous history and started again. Seen from above, the North American continent presented a *tableau vivant* of human experience from savagery to urbanity. Turner's third point grew out of the Census Bureau's announcement in 1890 that there no longer was a large area of free, open land. The unique social conditions that had given Americans their egalitarianism and their democracy had ended. A new (and probably darker) era loomed. Turner wrote in terms of continuous historical transitions and here was the final one.

Rebelling against Eurocentric ideas, Turner sought a strictly American explanation for American history. His essay was also a manifesto for the importance of his own region, which he wanted to understand in other than dime-novel terms. Turner did not write about morality or heroism. He offered an American version of the impersonal social conflict that Marx conceptualised around the notion of the class struggle. Yet Turner did make value judgments. One emerged consciously out of the place from which he came and the other unconsciously from the time in which he lived.

Turner's place was Wisconsin, which never has been part of the mythic West, but rather is dairy country, a middle ground between savagery and effeteness, a garden tamed out of wilderness. His time was the aftermath of the Civil War, when Yankees and Rebels joined hands and tried to forget the fundamental conflict over nationality, race and the conditions of labour that had ripped open the Republic. The former slaves were left to their fate beneath renewed white supremacy. As participants in the American story, they simply did not count. When the Republic celebrated its centennial with a great exhibition in Philadelphia, only a bust of Frederick Douglass reminded visitors of those Americans for whom the country's history meant not one century of independence but rather two and a half centuries of enslavement. Among white Americans, Northern and Southern alike, white supremacy and black and Native American people's exclusion from the main story were simply given. Turner did exclude both groups, black people and Native Americans, but he was not malign; he merely summed up what his age thought.

Unlike Turner, Stevens had always been sensitive to race. In *Giant* and *Anne Frank* he faced the issue of racism directly. But *Shane* preceded those films. It was released only a year before the Supreme Court's epochal decision outlawing segregation in *Brown vs. Board of Education of Topeka, Kansas* and two years before the emergence of Martin Luther King Jr. Schaefer's Shane is positively identified as a Mississippian by his courtliness and soft accent, in a tradition of Westerners who are also Southern instinctive gentlemen that reaches back to Owen Wister's *The Virginian*. Stevens often talked about filming Wister's novel and his Shane is indeed an instinctive gentleman. But the plain-folks Torrey takes on the burden of 'Southern honour'. He provokes his own death by calling Wilson 'a low-down, lying Yankee' after Wilson has said that 'Stonewall Jackson was trash himself, him and Lee and all the rest of them Rebs'. Like the Turner thesis, like any number of other Westerns and like the textbooks of its day, *Shane* construes the historical argument of Yankee and Rebel as a family quarrel to be left behind.

Decades after its presentation, the Turner thesis continued to form the very heart of historians' understanding of the West. It would have appealed to Stevens' instincts and temperament. There is no reason, though, to think that he had been exposed to it. Turner's essay is the sort of thing that Jack Schaefer would have read when he was teaching himself American history and certainly A. B. Guthrie would have known about it and taught it in his classes at Kentucky. In its way 'The Significance of the Frontier in American History' is as much a part of the literature of the West as Guthrie's *The Big Sky* or *Shane* itself. Jack Schaefer constructed his novel around Turnerian ideas. Guthrie's script gave those ideas the form that they take in the film, with the rancher and the farmer each having his chance to state his position in straight, open debate. Stevens realised that debate in a way that allowed multiple resonances to run through the sequence.

The confrontation between Ryker and Starrett takes place in moonlight (in fact, day-for-night) after the separate Independence Day celebrations. When the Starrett party arrives home the off-screen voice of Morgan Ryker announces that he will 'open the gate', and a cut reveals him inside the fence. His appearance is almost magical, since nothing had blocked the view as the family approached. Two quick cuts bring the wagon inside the gate where a two-shot reveals Rufe Ryker and Wilson, mounted and facing the approaching family. Rufe's polite 'Howdy,

Starrett' and 'Evening ma'am' belie that he is a trespasser and that Morgan has taken control of their gate. The space within the fence is Marion's particularly, and when we first met them the Rykers damaged her garden. The image of sexual violation is clear, though by no means overstated. Cuts back and forth place Shane and Wilson in apposition/opposition to each other.

Ryker makes his offer: he will buy Starrett out, hire him for top wages and let him run his cattle with the herd. His 'Is that fair?' provokes Starrett's response that the farmers have been 'in the right all along', which cues Ryker to state his position. In a long speech the rancher describes how people like him discovered the valley, wrested it from the Indians and defeated rustlers so that the farmers' cattle as well as theirs could be safe. Now people who had 'never had to rawhide it' were taking over, digging ditches and diverting scarce water. He concludes by asking whether 'the men who did the work have no rights?'.

There are fourteen cuts during the speech, to the gunmen, Joe and Marion, Joey and back to Ryker. Joe responds not with another speech but rather with a dialogue, putting a frame around Ryker's account of the valley's history. Trappers and Indian traders had gone before and now 'the government' has legitimised the settler claims and guaranteed their tenure. Ryker has spoken of the men who shared his great adventure, but they are 'mostly dead now'. He alone is left to speak their story and make their case. He alone will benefit if that case prevails. Starrett invokes 'the others', whose company he has just enjoyed at the get-together. But to Ryker those people and the promise of their future will have to go for the sake of his hold on the past. Joey has been watching wide-eyed, and Ryker's last ploy is to invite the child into a small boy's B-Western dream of going 'partners with me'. Joe understands that what Ryker offers is dependency not partnership. He interjects that the child 'isn't of age' and the exchange ends.

Ryker has had his say. Despite our knowledge that he has brought in Wilson to defeat the settlers, he has made a powerful case that unenclosed common space becomes property when human effort transforms it. In his case the transformation is from 'wilderness' to economically productive open range (though the Cheyennes he has displaced had other ideas). He has framed his argument in terms of the right to profit, rugged individualism, and the position that his way represents where the valley's historical development should stop. John Locke, the philosophical father of economic liberalism, could not have put it better.

Ryker and Starrett will not be together in the frame again, but Starrett has not finished. He returns to the valley's history and future as Torrey's funeral breaks up. Lewis prepares to depart. Howells (Martin Mason) will join him and a general flight will follow if they go. The debate resumes with Lewis taking Ryker's part. Joe begins to rally the settlers in the name of Torrey's bravery, with Shane in the frame. Lewis responds that the last time Starrett spoke that way Torrey was alive. Another man is in the shot, but he is unidentified and has no connection to Lewis. That pattern will be repeated throughout this sequence. As Starrett and Shane speak for solidarity, others who count are also on camera. As Lewis argues for departure, he is effectively alone.

Joe turns from Torrey's bravery to the theme of 'a regular settlement, a town with churches and schools'. Lewis counters by adding 'graveyards' and Joe sits down in admission of defeat. Shane takes up the argument, invoking 'something that means more to you than anything else, your families', with a cut to Joey in close-up. Shane distances himself from the farmers by speaking of *your* families, *your* children, *you* people and asking if *you* have 'nerve enough not to give it up', but he shares the frame with all three Starretts. Joe rises, pulling himself up both physically from his chair and emotionally from his despond. Who is Ryker 'to run *us* from *our* homes?'. Over a cut to seven people, including Howells, his spouse and their children, Joe adds that 'he only wants to grow his beef, we want to grow our families'. The children are in the foreground. A cut back to the Starretts and Shane lets Joe finish his case with 'God didn't make all this country just for one man like Ryker'. Lewis, still alone, ends the argument where it began: 'He's got it, though. That's what counts.'

The whole group sees that Lewis' abandoned homestead has been set on fire. 'That's *our* place', he says. His wife shares the frame, in the first of a series of shots that restore him to the community. She teases him about never having built a room for their daughters. The other settlers join Joe's insistence that the community will help Lewis rebuild. Lewis asks 'You'd do that for us?'. He invites the others to join him fighting the fire and most of them depart pell-mell. Two hold back, the somewhat cowardly Howells, who still wants to depart, and Shipstead, who will stay but who does not know what to do about Ryker.

By this point it is obvious that Joe is a future mayor or legislator. He has set the agenda and controlled the order of speaking in the settlers' meetings. His strength is that he can bring others around to his own position. None the less, he thinks that he can take the task of dealing with Ryker upon himself, alone, echoing the individualism that led Torrey to his death. He cannot. On his line 'if I have to kill him [Ryker]', a cut fills the frame with a close-up of Shane, who, unlike Starrett, can do it. The combination of line and shot reprises an earlier exchange between Ryker ('I like Starrett too, but I'll kill him if I have to') and his hired gun Wilson ('You mean I'll kill him if you have to').

The sequence ends with a bucket brigade at Lewis' place. It is the last we see of the farming community. They entered the narrative as perplexed individuals with no better idea about what to do in their crisis than to go to town together. They leave the narrative acting together. Joe's first premise in the debate with Ryker had been 'and us in the right all along'. Both of the points he made to the rancher, that his kind of people formed a community and that rightfulness was on their side, have now been realised. Ryker has not been defeated yet, but what he stands for will not mark the end of the valley's historical development.

One puzzle remains in the film's historical argument: Grafton, the storekeeper. Jack Schaefer understood that the farmers were immersed in

the commercial, acquisitive, self-improving world. As already noted, in the novel Shane first intervenes in Starrett's life by helping him to bargain with a price-gouging trader. Stevens understood this too. Grafton's commercial establishment is the valley's neutral ground, although each group has its own entrance and its own space. The store links the farmers to the world of commerce. Within it Lewis' daughter tries on hats, Marion examines a mason jar and wonders 'What will they think of next?' and Joe flips through a catalogue, looking at pictures of derby hats and ladies in long-johns. Grafton sells work clothes to Shane, orders barbed wire for Starrett and outfits 'all those farmers'.

Grafton also mediates between the farmers and the cattlemen. The storekeeper declares Joe and Shane the victors in their fist fight against the Ryker crowd. He tells Rufe that he 'likes Joe Starrett'. When the killing of Torrey is being set up, Wilson has to make it 'look right for Grafton'. Grafton makes moral judgments, for example, when he spots Will the bartender sneaking a flask of whisky to Lewis. Yet he cannot resolve any issue that counts. As the fist fight demolishes his bar room, Morgan tells him, 'You keep out of this' and 'Stop buttin' in'. Paul McVey's acting makes the character hesitant and nervous. He disappears from the narrative before the killing of Torrey, leaving Will to act as his surrogate at the final confrontation between Shane and the Rykers ('Will, you're a witness to this', says Ryker). Commerce may have been the driving force of nineteenth-century development, but the film remains fundamentally uncertain about its significance.

In one of his more evocative passages, Frederick Jackson Turner invited his readers to place themselves imaginatively at the Appalachian pass where Virginia tumbles into Kentucky in about 1770, as Daniel Boone's people are passing. 'Stand at Cumberland Gap,' he wrote, 'and watch the procession of civilization marching single file – the buffalo following the trail to the salt springs, the Indian, the fur-trader and hunter, the cattle raiser, the pioneer farmer – and the frontier has passed. Stand at South Pass in the Rockies a century later and see the same procession, with wider intervals between.' This farming community near South Pass has decided not to move on but rather to stay, to help Lewis recover and to complete the task of turning the valley into 'farming country'. It will not let itself be scattered into helpless individuals. The frontier has passed. Ryker rather than the farmers should move, if he can find any place to go.

8

. . . .

MEN WITH FISTS AND GUNS

The debate about history is resolved once the farmers make the collective decision to stay. *Shane*'s parallel dramas about violence between men, illicit attraction between a man and a woman and what place a wanderer can have in a world of families and settlement remain to be considered. Let us take violence first. Of all these topics, it was the one foremost on Stevens' mind. As he explained at Ohio State University in 1973:

> We had a shooting...that we wanted to make something out of, because the film was really about shooting. The film was really for the deglamorizing of the six-shooter that was becoming a graceful object in the fictional hands of the illustrators and particularly the film people. And it was a time, I remember, when kids had gone very Western. There were Western chaps and hats and cap guns everywhere.... We wanted to put the six-gun in its place, visually, in a period, as a dangerous weapon. And we did.

The violence in *Shane* has to be seen through the eyes of Joey and from the perspective that, as he encounters fighting and killing, he grows. It must also be seen in terms of his confrontation with growing up male in a harsh world. Though the film's narrative covers only a few weeks, Joey is a much wiser person by the end.

The child has a rifle when we first meet him; he would kill the deer browsing near the homestead if he could. When he and Shane first speak, Joey cannot see Shane's pistol. The next shot puts the weapon into the child's field of vision. That motivates Joey to leap down from the fence, run to the pump behind Shane, rifle in hand and to cock the rifle as Shane starts to drink the water. Joey's words after Shane draws are 'I just wanted you to see my rifle. Bet you can shoot', and then hesitantly, 'can't you?'. As the Ryker party approaches, Joe takes the rifle and, unlike his son, he does point it at Shane. The two men's tussle of will about whether Shane leaves with a gun pointed at him or goes by his own choice prefigures their eventual confrontation over which one of them will go to town at the film's end. Joey watches it all.

When Shane returns and proclaims himself a 'friend of Starrett's' his gun is prominently placed and the reaction shot shows that Ryker has noticed it. As Shane himself will later say of Wilson, this armed man in buckskin is 'no cowpuncher', or farmhand either. Shane joins the family for supper and while Joe makes his speech about farming replacing herding, Joey squats behind Shane's chair, fascinated by the holstered pistol hanging on it. Joe drops a hint that he would welcome Shane staying on and Joey rocks back and forth almost compulsively in a rocking-chair, unable to contain the tension that Shane's arrival has set up in him. After supper, when Shane goes out to chop the tree stump, Joey worries that he might be leaving without saying good-bye. Joe reassures him by pointing at the pistol: 'He wouldn't go without taking that.'

Joey's next encounter with the gun question happens the following dawn when he discovers the deer browsing in his mother's garden. Now he does more than point the weapon. His spoken 'Bang! Bang!' and his wish that 'they'd get me some bullets for this gun' start the film's escalation towards its two real shooting scenes. His play-shooting also wakes Shane. Speaking for both parents, Joey invites Shane to stay. Speaking for himself, he asks to be taught to shoot, knowing that Shane is more likely than his father to do it. After Shane accepts the invitation to stay, the boy hurls himself onto a bed his mother is making in sheer physical delight.

When Shane goes to town to get barbed wire, work clothes and soda pop, Joey runs behind him for a moment, prefiguring the way in which he follows Shane into town at the film's end. He gets his rifle out again, play-shoots 'Rykers' and asks his father for a shooting lesson, as if to give Joe a last chance while Shane is away. The boy has noticed that Shane did not take his gun. Joe counters that he himself doesn't wear one to town. Joey's precocious response sums up the difference between the two men: 'It goes with him, though.' Joey has seen his father and Shane bond on Joe's ground as they defeated the tree stump. As father and son finish their conversation, Joey wants to know how the two would do on Shane's. 'Could you whip him, Pa? Could you whip Shane?' he asks. For the moment, the question has to go unanswered.

Joey gets a partial answer during the bar-room fist fight, as Shane and his father take on the Rykers. The sequence is very long, running nearly seven minutes from the moment Shane tosses two whiskys over Chris Calloway to Grafton's declaration that Shane and Starrett have won. There are approximately seventy shots in the first phase of the fight and about eighty in the second. Nineteen shots show Joey watching the

Joey examines Shane's pistol

Joey tells Shane the Starretts wish he would stay

Shane knocks Chris out

Shane and Joe take on the Rykers

action. Two show Joey and Marion watching together, after Joe has joined the fray and two more show Marion watching alone. All the other settlers stay away, men and women alike, even though the men have scorned Shane for his earlier refusal to fight Chris.

The fight begins slowly, as Shane and Calloway take each other's measure. But after Joe enters the cutting becomes very quick, with a number of shots that last only fractions of a second. Multiple camera positions (despite the cumbersome equipment Stevens had to use) shift the point of view constantly, conveying the disorientation and confusion of a bar-room brawl. Shane's first punch sends Chris flying into the store, leaving the cowboy bloody and dazed, exactly as Stevens envisioned when he first marked up the novel ('make Chris face up between cuts he goes behind the table and comes up with a bloody face').

By the fight's conclusion three separate purposes have been achieved. One is to complete the bonding between Joe and Shane. The second is to resolve Joey's doubts about his father – at fist fighting, the two men are clearly a match, even though they have fought (this time) as allies rather than opponents. The third is to insist that punches hurt, foreshadowing Stevens' later insistence that bullets do terrible damage. Joey, however, has not yet understood that point. Back at the farm, as Marion begins to treat the two men's bruises, he rocks back and forth in delight at what he has seen. Given that Marion thinks both men were 'wonderful', the boy's enjoyment need not be treated as a problem. But it does confirm the train of thought that was already in Joey's mind at Shane's arrival: to be a man is to fight.

Joey is still fascinated by Shane's gun and his next chance to learn is the shooting lesson. Joey has been watching Shane put up barbed wire and the boy forces the topic of fighting, asking Shane what he would do if he caught somebody cutting the wire. Shane tries to duck it, responding that he would ask them politely to go around by the gate. They race back to the barn and Joey will not let the topic go. Why doesn't Shane wear his six-shooter, he wants to know. He confesses that he has looked at Shane's gun, hidden in his bedroll and holds Shane to his promise to teach him to shoot.

Ladd brings a brief look of pain and doubt to his character's face, as if Shane is remembering a life-defining moment in his own youth. None the less, he grants Joey's wish. He shows him how to fast-draw, tells him about different gunfighters' techniques, offers the value judgment that one gun is all a man needs if he knows how to use it and finally draws his own gun and shoots at a rock. Unobserved by the gunman and the boy, Marion sees it all. She intervenes after he fires, because she doesn't want guns to be her boy's life. When Shane responds that a gun is only a tool, as good or as bad as the person wielding it, her answer is irrefutable: there ought to be no guns left in the valley, including Shane's.

The shooting lesson is the point where Stevens first uses noticeable sound effects. The noise that we hear when Shane fast-draws, shoots at the stone and sends it flying, is not the crack of a handgun: it's a howitzer, blasting its blank shot into a garbage can for added reverberation, with a rifle bullet's whine mixed in. One result is to convey the boy's own excited, subjective sense of the favour that Shane has done for him. Another, however, is to signal that the film's argument about firearms has moved to a different level. Stevens reinforces the point when Marion shoos the boy away. 'Bang! Bang!' he says, play-firing his wooden pistol. He has said that before, but now Stevens uses an echo chamber, which gives the boy's high, childish voice something of the surreal timbre that the howitzer-and-rifle effect gave to Shane's pistol. Whether the echo in Joey's voice represents the boy's own excitement or stands for what Marion fears about her son's

future is left unstated. But the emotional stakes have been raised and a new aesthetic device has been introduced. Shane's shot at the rock and Joey's imitation of it will reverberate through the rest of the film.

After the bar-room fight Ryker had promised that the next time there is a settler/cattleman fight 'the air is gonna be filled with gunsmoke'. Though Shane and the homesteaders don't know it, Wilson has arrived in the valley. In the next tavern sequence, during the cowboys' Fourth of July

The shooting lesson

celebration, Torrey sets himself up to be the victim of a real shooting. His murder is at the very heart of the picture and it is the only moment of violence when the point of view is not Joey's. Instead, the witness is Shipstead, the brave but decidedly unviolent Swede. Torrey's death requires the closest analysis, both because of Steven's intentions for the film and because it marks a breaking point in the Western genre's entire aesthetic and politics of violence.

A dissolve into daylight out of the night-time debate between Starrett and Ryker introduces Torrey and Shipstead riding towards town: Torrey is in the foreground astride a horse that seems to be as diminutive as himself. Deeper in the frame, the Swede seems to tower above him. 'Dixie' is on the soundtrack, played slowly by deep strings and woodwinds in a minor key. The sequence was shot in bad weather and there are rumbles of thunder throughout. In front of Grafton's, and between it and the blacksmith shop where Shipstead is going, there is a morass of thick, dark mud (which was created by watering the street overnight, after Stevens decided that the wetting it had already received did not give a powerful enough effect). Torrey's own persona and the use of 'Dixie' conjure up a strong image of Southern honour, the absolute determination on one man's part that no other man will push him around. The music, the threatening weather and the highly visible mud all indicate where Torrey's allowing a thoughtless adherence to honour to define his life, without regard to either common sense or his own responsibilities, is taking him.

Inside Grafton's bar the two Ryker brothers plot with Wilson on how to get Starrett to confront them. Killing Torrey is Wilson's idea, after Morgan spots the two settlers arriving. One settler has already run, the gunfighter reasons, and a death will stampede the rest. As the two riders approach, Wilson and Morgan take up positions on the saloon porch, each in a classic pose of men with nothing better to do than hang out and wait for trouble. Wilson leans on the saloon's wall and Morgan sits down in a chair. They do not move as the pair ride past. Torrey and Shipstead dismount and tie up their horses. Wilson steps away from the wall and walks slowly towards the camera along the boardwalk in front of Grafton's, perhaps a foot above ground level. He is almost centre frame, growing in screen size relative to the foreground figures as he walks, until he reaches the end of the building where the boardwalk ends. He steps left, leans against the building and challenges Torrey with 'Hey! Come here!'

It is the same device that Stevens used much earlier to introduce the settler Ernie Wright arriving on his buckboard to announce his departure, while Joe and Joey talk about Shane. Two actions are happening at once and the action emerging from the background will outweigh and displace whatever is happening in the foreground. Stevens will use the device again in a few moments, when the Swede approaches the Starrett homestead with Torrey's dead body while Shane and Starrett converse. The camera is absolutely still during all three shots, without any movement or special use of the lens to emphasise the emergence of the background action.

Torrey is not somebody to decline a challenge. As he responds to Wilson, the camera is on his level, down in the mud. It pans and tracks with him as he picks his way tentatively and clumsily towards the gunfighter. Wilson blocks him when he tries to step up to the boardwalk, emphasising the difference between his height and Torrey's. Wilson walks back along the boardwalk and Torrey parallels him on the ground, while the long tracking shot continues. Wilson steps up from in front of the store to the higher porch in front of the saloon. Torrey is still mired in the mud but now Wilson towers over him. His position is given extra

Torrey's death

solidity from beneath by the huge round timbers on which the saloon rests. The viewpoint shifts up to the saloon porch as the fatal exchange begins about 'Southern trash'. Three shots show Torrey from the level of Wilson's gunbelt. In the first two, the camera is at Wilson's left, behind the pistol he will not use. These are intercut with shots from Torrey's viewpoint looking up at Wilson. In the third shot from the porch, when Torrey moves to draw and Wilson whips out his pistol, the camera is again at holster level, but this time on the gunman's right, behind the pistol he is going to use.

With both men's guns drawn, Stevens cuts to Shipstead's perspective, although much closer than where the Swede is actually standing. Knowing he is going to die, Torrey hesitantly raises his pistol, his arm seeming to shake as he does. Wilson fires and the howitzer special effect is used once again. Torrey has been wired from the back and he is jerked down into the mud, falling onto a hidden mattress while the mud splashes into his face. Stevens' intention was to break the Western's long-standing convention that a gunshot death is clean, a matter of death without cruelty. He wanted to show what happens to a man's body when a high-calibre slug hits it. There is no fast cutting to convey subjective excitement or to draw viewers in. Instead, only four set-ups are used during the whole exchange between Wilson's 'Hey!' and Torrey's fall. The slow movement of the sequence takes us into Torrey's own growing awareness that he cannot escape. It also makes Wilson a cold-blooded man who knows exactly what he is doing and does not care about the consequences. There is nothing glamorous or heroic about Torrey's death. It is just the squalid waste of a human life, taken callously as the victim waits in terror.

The horror of the situation is apparent the evening after Torrey's funeral. Grafton, the settlers and most of the Rykers now are out of the narrative. The only figures who will count from this point to the end are the three Starretts, Shane, the two Ryker brothers, Calloway and Wilson. Immense tensions are running among the four people at the Starrett homestead. Ryker's men arrive to invite Starrett to talk peace at Grafton's. Joe greets them as he greeted the first Ryker party, with a rifle in his hands. This time it is his, not Joey's, and it is loaded. As they talk, Shane covers him with his pistol, while Joey watches. Chris Calloway arrives with his news for Shane that Joe is being set up.

Joey begins to play-shoot and the echo chamber is used at every 'Bang!'. In the next few shots Joey lets loose a flood of manic little-boy energy, dancing and play-shooting his way around the homestead exterior. The Bang! Bang! continues, the volume rising and falling while Joe and Marion talk frantically inside. Joey bursts into the house: 'Bang! Bang! Bang! Bang! Bang!' His own frenzy raises his mother's anxiety to the same level, until she sends him to 'go outside and play'.

His play-shooting, that is no longer child's play, finally stops. It has been a very powerful exposition of the psychological damage that exposure to the adult world of violence can wreak upon the innocent and the young. Without question, Stevens' wartime experience would have exposed him to children suffering the trauma of war. When he made *Shane*, the caring professions were decades away from their current understanding that witnessing physical violence brings psychological trauma, especially to children. But his direction of Joey and his use of the echo chamber at this point in the film suggest that he already understood the point.

The second fist fight follows. It pits Joe against Shane in a confrontation that was predictable from their first meeting. It also breaks the anxiety at the homestead. Dressed once more in buckskins and wearing his pistol, Shane comes to the cabin door to stop Joe from going to town. Despite Ladd's smaller stature, the camera angle and the positioning of the actors make him and Heflin seem equal. After brief verbal sparring, Joe charges Shane in an convulsive release of pent-up tension. Unlike Shane's fight with Chris, there is no taking each other's measure. Each knows the other well, and it becomes a wild mêlée of wrestling, slugging, tripping and pushing. It only takes two minutes from Joe's opening lunge at Shane standing in the doorway to the moment when Shane, pinned by the bigger man against the tree stump, draws his pistol and knocks Joe out. Yet the sequence seems as long and as packed as the earlier seven minute sequence beginning with Shane tossing whisky at Chris and ending with Grafton pronouncing Starrett and Shane the victors.

There are fifty-six shots during the fight sequence. Though the two men begin brawling immediately, the editing gives the same effect of building to a furious pace that was used in the first fight scene at the saloon. A mere two shots account for the first twenty-five seconds of screen time, both are taken from inside the cabin showing Marion's and Joey's reactions. Hers counts particularly, as she dashes from window to window while the two men slam each other back and forth. There is a crescendo of animal-noise sound effects, and the cattle and horses rear up in fright. As in the first fight, Stevens intercuts to the witnesses. Joey, his own tensions already more or less spent with the play-shooting, remains fairly still. As the men fight each other to a standstill until Shane uses his pistol butt to win, the boy realises that in a fair fight the two men are even and that perhaps his father is better. His choice of which one to emulate must depend on their respective virtues rather than on the fighting prowess of either, which complicates his sense of being a man. That is precisely what Shane means when he tells Marion after the fight is over that 'nobody can blame [Joe] for not keeping that appointment'. The only persons who could have blamed him are Joe himself and little Joey. Neither will do so.

None the less, Joey still does not grasp the point of Shane's confrontation with his father, which is that Joe could not possibly win at Grafton's and that there is no point in going to a death like Torrey's. The issue has been too serious for fighting clean. At Joey's next line – 'Shane, you hit him with your gun! I hate you!' – Stevens uses the echo chamber again. When Shane departs a moment later to keep Joe's date, Marion helps the boy to understand that he does not hate Shane. Joey runs after

Shane and Joe brawl over who should go to town

him, reprising the way that he first ran behind the wagon when Shane went to town to buy work clothes.

The two Ryker brothers and Wilson are waiting in the saloon. In one carefully crafted wordless shot that begins with a short pan left and turns into a long pan right, Stevens positions all three where they will be when Shane enters. The short pan places Wilson with his back against one wall. Carrying a rifle, Morgan mounts the stairs to the balcony. As he disappears through the top of the frame, the slow pan right continues, following Rufe Ryker until he turns around and sits down. He is about to preside over what he thinks will be Starrett's destruction and at no point in the film is his persona of an outmoded pagan god more pronounced than here. The sure, triumphant way that Emile Meyer carries himself in the shot conveys strong overtones of hubris.

Destruction is coming and Shane is the righteous nemesis who bears its cup. As he rides towards the town and Joey pursues him on foot, the music on the soundtrack is not his own theme but rather a variation on Wilson's pounding tympani, intermingled with major key chords, played predominantly by the brass instruments. Shane enters the town by the same route Torrey and Shipstead had taken, passing as they did between trees that had been planted to serve as portals. Stevens uses virtually the same set-ups, signalling that Shane is taking not only Joe's place but also Torrey's.

Shane goes straight in through the exterior saloon door. Neither he nor anybody else from the settler community has used it previously, except for Joe, who charged through it to rescue Shane from the Rykers during the saloon fight. The inside first shot has him sharing the frame with Wilson. A card player, previously not seen, leaves as soon as Shane enters and Wilson shifts his signature coffee pot so that it will not be in his way. Joey arrives to take up his role as witness to what the adults do.

It takes a few seconds short of three minutes from Shane's announcement to Ryker that he has come to get his offer to Morgan's fall from the balcony, becoming the final member of the malign trio to die. During that time Stevens reprises various visual devices that he has used already. Joey peers from beneath the saloon's half-doors, just as he did during the fist fight. A second card player slinks out. So does the saloon dog, repeating what it had done when Wilson first arrived. Wilson advises Shane not to push too far, which is precisely what Shane had told Chris at their first meeting in the same place. The two men repeat dialogue compressed from Wilson's exchange with Torrey, with Wilson taking several lines that the Southerner had spoken earlier. 'So you're Jack Wilson' ('So you're Stonewall Torrey'). 'I've heard about you.' 'What have you heard, Shane?' 'I've heard that you're a low-down Yankee liar,' which had been Torrey's final words before Wilson's 'Prove it' provoked him to draw.

'Prove it,' says Wilson again. But this time Wilson is seated, looking up to a self-confident Shane, rather than standing on a porch above his outclassed victim. As in the first shooting, Wilson clears his holster first. Shane dispatches both him and Ryker in one fast move, twirls his gun and holsters it. He draws it again fast enough to deal with Morgan when Joey shouts a warning. Even with this, Stevens is reprising. The innocent but alert Joey of just a few weeks before had spotted Shane far down the valley and had warned his father that somebody was coming. Shane had complimented him on it then. This much wiser child is even more alert and saves Shane's life. He has just watched the death of one man, Ryker, who briefly offered himself to the boy as a role model. But he still has to face the question of whether it's Shane or Joe who offers the model for his own future.

Wilson's death

9

. . . .

MARION'S AWAKENING

What Joe has and Shane lacks is Marion. Throughout his career, Stevens was interested in women's relationship to a male-dominated world, including his own world of film production. Talking in 1973 at Ohio State University, he noted that if the actors in a director's film 'can't act at all, he's in trouble and – pardon me, he or she is in trouble, who is directing'. At that point there were even fewer women directing Hollywood films than there are today.

Even in Stevens' pre-Second World War comedy period, the women in his films are remarkably strong characters, from Katharine Hepburn's *Alice Adams* to the same actress's figure of intelligent glamour in *Woman of the Year*. Stevens' women are hardly ever portrayed simply as domestic. They entertain audiences and they fire guns (Barbara Stanwyck in *Annie Oakley*). They give dance lessons and enjoy New York night life (Ginger Rogers in *Swing Time*). They work in factories or they live the free lives that a factory owner's daughter can enjoy (Shelley Winters and Elizabeth Taylor, respectively, in *A Place in the Sun*). They are heroic martyrs (Millie Perkins as Anne Frank). Even when a central female figure is married, the marriage has its complications. The women played by Irene Dunne in *Penny Serenade* (1941) and Elizabeth Taylor in *Giant* are two such instances. Marion is another.

Modern-day historians have recovered what pioneering exacted from women: the separation from family and society, the isolation of farm and ranch life, the loss of creature comforts on the trail and in sod houses. One account shows a colossal rate of women's depression, insanity, psychosomatic illness and death in a supposedly idyllic Wisconsin community. To survive took great strength. Stevens would have seen that kind of strength in his own mother during her California vaudeville career. Novelist Schaefer and scriptwriter Guthrie may well have encountered the sources about Western women that more recent historians have exploited. Whatever way Stevens, Schaefer and Guthrie derived Marion, they and Jean Arthur present her as a woman of considerable character and depth.

Arthur's own input is worth considering. In later accounts she described Stevens' insistence that she play Marion as a tired, faded figure, from whom ten years of pioneer marriage had taken a lot, 'and it was very difficult for me'. From her point of view, 'you feel sorry for these little people...the heavies [were] the most interesting people in the picture'. She described her difficulties working with Alan Ladd. His not having even heard of Stevens before *Shane* made her think that 'he lacked the capability of really knowing. He should have known who George Stevens was, you know.' She bemoaned the actor's sensitivity 'about his lack of height. And you couldn't kid around about it.' Although their characters' mutual attraction is palpable, there was no off-screen magnetism between them. She was unhappy with the way that her old friend Stevens had become 'serious, very serious, no jokes. It was like I never knew him before ... it was very sad.' Others on the production have described her aloofness and how she would go off into the Grand Tetons during location shooting. The power that the actress brings to Marion's discontent and her eventual explosion of anger about her fate came from deep within Arthur herself.

The choice to costume Marion in trousers for her introduction is not historically accurate but it does suggest the extent to which frontier life has desexualised her. From the start, Shane renews her energy. We first see her full-length in a quick cut when she comes out of the house. Two shots later she and Shane join Joe and Joey in the frame simultaneously, as if to balance each other. She raises the idea that Shane might stay, suggesting that Joe invite the stranger to supper. When Joe asks Shane 'where you're bound?' and Shane replies 'Some place I've never been', he glances at her. Three shots follow of the wanderer and the farmwife looking at each other, while her theme music is played by string instruments. Joe speaks of needing a hired hand and Shane glances at Marion again. After she serves dessert, Joe comments on her getting out the 'good plates and extra forks'. There is a tablecloth as well. Joe senses that the comment has disturbed her and asks 'what's the matter, Marion?'. Her response is 'nothing' as she looks away from him, her theme still playing. Shane's compliment on her 'elegant dinner' gives a faint echo of the character's ability in the novel to talk about fashion and suggests that he senses her frustrations.

After Joey tells Shane that both his parents hope he will stay on, she appears in a dress. It is plain and gray, in keeping with the subdued earth-tone colours in which Stevens costumed all the settlers. But it begins a feminine counterpoint, expressed through her costuming before she shapes it into words, to the escalation of the firearms theme. Marion does wear trousers one more time, when the settler men gather. When they go to town for supplies she appears in a graceful mid-calf A-line skirt, a dark blue top and a gold headband. She is carrying a hat. She has made the others wait and she asks if Joe can expect her to be 'ready in the time it takes to hitch up a team'. None of the other settler women are as well dressed. As Joe makes a patronising speech to Shane about the need for a married man to appreciate his woman, Shane glances away, almost guiltily.

Her next big scene follows that evening, as she tends the two men's cuts and bruises after the bar-room fight. Most of the action takes place during one two-minute take, with the camera absolutely still except for an almost imperceptible pan. The set is the Starrett living room, with a door to the left leading outside and the parents' and child's bedroom doors in the background.

During the take, there are twelve impeccably timed and choreographed actions, beginning comically with a mock 'ouch' from Shane when Marion puts turpentine on his wounded forehead. Joe and Joey go into their respective bedrooms, converting the family group into a two-shot of Marion and Shane. Joey re-emerges and asks his mother to come into his room. Behind the closed door, but fully audible and somewhat amplified with an echo chamber, he tells her that 'I just love Shane'. Shane hears it, stands and exits. Marion re-enters the room and gazes after him. Joe re-enters. Marion goes to him, the camera panning slightly with her. She asks Joe to 'Hold me, don't say anything, just hold me', and they go into their bedroom together. From behind his door, Joey calls out goodnight to each of them and each responds. The take finishes as the boy shouts 'Goodnight, Shane'. This time the echo chamber is used emphatically, foreshadowing Joey's anguished cries at the end of the film. There follows a fade to black.

The next stage in Marion's development is intercut with the shooting lesson. As Joey watches Shane, a dissolve reveals her indoors wearing a jaunty hat, with her theme music playing. She is taking dresses out of her trunk, holding each one up to herself and putting it aside. A warm smile crosses her face as she bends and takes out something white. A dissolve takes us back to Shane and Joey. We see her next outdoors, wearing the full-skirted lacy dress that she has taken out of the trunk. Joe is not about and it seems that she wants to show it off to Shane. Instead

Marion and Joey in her garden

Marion tells Shane that 'we understand'

Joe sees Marion gazing after Shane

Marion takes her wedding dress out of her trunk

she comes upon the shooting lesson and confronts Shane on the subject of guns. When Joe rides up we learn that the dress is her wedding gown. She will wear it to the settlers' Independence Day party, which will also honour their tenth anniversary. Clearly she is experiencing something like the surge of emotions that the nineteenth-century feminist writer Kate Chopin described in her great novel of frustrated American womanhood, *The Awakening*.

The confusion about Marion's feelings is raised again during the settlers' dance. More obviously than any other footage, the dance was filmed on a soundstage and the artificiality of the setting is striking. In the first shot, Joe and Marion move very sedately together, deep in the background. Torrey arrives from town and the music speeds up as the dance finishes. Now Marion is much closer to the camera, though she is separated from it by the fence and bushes that enclose the dancing space. Her partner's face cannot be seen, but his blue costume shows that Joe (who is wearing brown in the sequence) has metamorphosed into Shane. In all probability, the change is just a small anomaly that Stevens chose to ignore, but it does express the complexities that are being worked out.

During the next few shots the community honours the couple's anniversary. Joe is already in centre frame, but Marion has to be called forward. Shane walks into the frame with her. Arthur plays her character's part absolutely straight, looking warmly at Joe. But when the little ceremony ends she glances over to Shane and Joey. Which one, the hired hand or her son, is she looking at? Does she herself know? Shane is her partner as the dancing resumes at a livelier pace than before. Joe watches without concern. As he will tell her later, it takes him time to see things.

During the evening sequence between Torrey's funeral and the second fight, when both his and her tensions burst forth, we finally learn that he has seen and understood. To appreciate the couple's moment of crisis, it may help to look beyond the film. By the time *Shane* was made, Stevens' marriage to his first wife Yvonne had been over for years, a casualty of his work habits. The two remained close, living in apartments in the same building and Yvonne Stevens betrayed no bitterness when she was interviewed many years later for the George Stevens Oral History collection. She was at Jackson Hole for much of the location shooting. For his part, George Stevens once borrowed the title of one of his own films by calling marriage 'the only game in town' to characterise relations

Joe and Marion at the picnic

Shane and Marion dancing

between men and women. Expanding and complicating that theme in an interview, he called marriage:

> the greatest of all human – I'll say human problems. You know the problem of the male and female relationship.... Now, the only solution we know in our community is marriage and marriage takes much else with it. It means a lifetime of companionship and association, you know, not just for the purpose of bearing a child. So to protect the child, to conceive the child, you need a lifetime of association.

Stevens understood the pressures placed on a marriage by a society that values glamour and wealth. The Starretts are a very ordinary couple. Joe is content with his lot, but something within Marion wants more. We can sense her feelings from a comment Stevens made about the Montgomery Clift/Shelley Winters pairing in *A Place in the Sun*. Referring to the scene in which Clift's George Eastman listens to his pregnant factory-worker girlfriend tell him how wonderful their future together will be, Stevens paraphrased it as: '"Jesus, we could be just like other married people. You know, me and my pedal pushers, you know and I could push the kids out of the way of the stove and I could cook up slop for you and you'd be working like a son of a bitch, you know and you'd be glad you had a...", and she's telling him this, which is just where he came from, which is purely unreal.'

Stevens began working on *Shane* while he was finishing *A Place in the Sun*. Though he denied making a deliberate trilogy, it seems reasonable to trace a continuity from Eastman's frustrations to Marion's repression.

Marion's confrontation with Joe begins after Torrey's funeral as Joe is saddling up to confront Ryker. Wearing the skirt and top that first signified her emergence from drudgery, she tries to stop him. 'Joe, you can't do it, go in town and kill Ryker, he'll kill you,' she pleads. A cut transports us to Grafton's, where Ryker is confirming her point at that very moment: 'Tell him I'm a reasonable man, tell him I'm beat, tell him anything. But by Jupiter! get him here.' Another cut takes us back to the farm and she repeats her previous line, 'Joe, he'll *kill* you.' Shane is in the room, avoiding their quarrel while he teaches Joey about a 'false square knot' that 'won't hold'. He refuses to intervene when she asks. Joe does not

Marion confronts Joe

even respond to her request to 'please wait, won't you do even this for me?'.

After the 'peace party' has left she tells Joe (correctly) that he doesn't really believe they have 'gone home'. Joe makes a short speech about 'all the things that will be' provoking an ironic 'will be' from her. Joey bursts in, firing his play pistol at both parents. Marion takes on the issue of men's destructive, violent 'pride, a silly kind of a pride', exactly the pride that had Torrey killed. She asks Joe whether she or Joey really mean anything to him. If he dies, he responds, she will be taken care of, maybe even better then he could do himself. Joe is no fool. Wilson will be at Grafton's, which means that his going to town will be as much a suicide mission as Torrey's. The difference is that Torrey never understood either himself or the situation and Joe fully comprehends both. Marion hides her face, as if in shame.

Meanwhile Shane has received Calloway's warning that Joe is 'up against a stacked deck'. He enters the farmhouse, wearing his buckskins. This is his, Shane's, 'kind of game' and Joe is 'no match for Wilson'. Marion finally snaps. Both men are out of their senses. Was it worth a life for 'this shack, this little piece of ground and nothing but work, work, work?'. She is sick of it. Joe's response is chilling. She doesn't mean what she has said, but 'even if that was the truth, it wouldn't change things'. Her values and his could hardly be farther apart. It takes Joe's defeat by Shane and Shane's irrevocable departure to guarantee that Joe will live and the couple will stay together.

Joe has told Marion that he knows she is drawn to another. She has mocked his freehold-farmer dreams. He has responded that her opinion does not count. The hurtful things have been said. How the couple will feel about each other now can only be left open. Like all of Stevens' female characters, Marion is no stereotype, no cardboard cut-out. She is a good person, but she has also learned about herself and she has tried hard to act upon what she now knows. She points directly towards the crisis of relations between the sexes that was not far off from happening in American society. The tensions within the Starrett homestead do not tear it apart. On the contrary, Marion conveys her own stance about what to do with moving restraint, when she shakes Shane's hand as she bids him farewell. But those tensions do account for Joe's furious energy as he hurls himself at Shane.

10

· ·

LONERS AND OUTSIDERS

Outsiders appear throughout George Stevens' work, from Hepburn's Alice Adams, through Fred Astaire's 'Lucky' in *Swing Time*, to Elizabeth Taylor's Leslie Benedict and James Dean's Jett Rink in *Giant*. The line culminates, perhaps, in Max von Sydow's Jesus in *The Greatest Story Ever Told*. Stevens developed a repertoire of actions and shots to show the discomfort of a person who does not belong. Katharine Hepburn's Alice Adams enters her first society gathering with the same hesitance that Montgomery Clift's George Eastman displays at his in *A Place in the Sun*, despite the gap of time and experience on Stevens' part between the two films, and despite the former being a comedy and the latter a drama. Hardly any film character could be less sure of himself than Torrey when he steps into the saloon to 'get a jug' on the Fourth of July, until Grafton encourages him to 'come on in'. In no respect was Spencer Tracy's screen persona akin to Elisha Cook Jr's, yet in *Woman of the Year* Stevens gives Tracy's plain-folks sportwriter exactly the same moves when the actor encounters Hepburn's high-flying columnist in the office of their newspaper's editor.

Shane may provide the most complex treatment of the outsider theme in all Stevens' work. Four characters – Shane, Wilson, Torrey and Chris Calloway – have outsider qualities. During the film they dance a quadrille of shifting positions. In addition, Stevens considers the problem of belonging to an unworthy community, through the medium of Chris, Wilson and their employer Ryker.

For all the rancher's thrashing about as the world changes around him, Ryker is not an outsider. Loyalty is his prime virtue. 'Nobody messes up one of my boys and gets away with it,' he tells Shane during the bar-room fight. He has an abstract sense of what is right, delivering his speech about cattlemen from the heart. Reducing his code to its minimum, Torrey's killing must 'look right for Grafton'. Ryker is a historically tragic figure as much as a villain, which may be what Jean Arthur meant with her comment that 'the heavies were wonderful'.

Ryker's great flaw is to hire Wilson, who is a loner rather than an outsider. He has no code, only a reputation and a skill. Shane recognises 'a man named Wilson' from Torrey's skimpy description at the picnic:

'Kinda lean. Decked out like a gunfighter. Packs two guns. Wears a black hat.' One settler knows the name: 'Jack Wilson? Gunfighter out of Cheyenne?' Wilson has a name, but no place or family. Cheyenne is not his home, it is where he has come from. 'Who'd they name you for, or would you know?' Torrey taunts him just before the shooting. He does not even join the Ryker group. Close to the end Morgan is still calling him 'the Stranger'. His coffee drinking is the sign of a professional who must keep his brain clear. But it also separates him from the cattlemen's ritual whisky drinking. He comes close to Dante's description in *The Inferno* of Satan's and Judas' frozen isolation as the worst condition at the bottom of Hell.

Wilson's relation to Shane is not villainy versus heroism, or dark clothes versus buckskin. Both are gunfighters, but Shane understands himself. He yearns to obtain what he cannot have and still be able to express his best qualities. To appreciate him fully we need to look at Torrey and Chris who stand between the two gunmen. Unlike Wilson and Shane, who are limited by identities they cannot shake, these two move past each other on opposite courses. Torrey is warm-hearted but he abandons his group and dies. Chris also separates himself from where he belongs. Unlike Torrey, he finds salvation by doing it.

Torrey's problem is not that he is Southern. Ever since *The Virginian*, the West had been the classic place in American fiction where the north–south divide could be healed. Historically an Alabamian probably would have followed his own latitude to Texas rather than go north to Wyoming, but the settlers are eclectic. They include the cowardly Ernie Wright, the slovenly Fred Lewis as well as the stoically brave Joe Starrett. The token immigrant Shipstead makes the speech that honours the Starretts' anniversary. He also leads the Lord's Prayer over Torrey's coffin. Starrett, their moral leader, does not judge the others for being what they are, not even Ernie who leaves the valley.

But Torrey will not accept the constraint that goes with belonging. He arrives late for the settlers' meeting. He gets 'thirsty' and goes into town ahead of the shopping expedition. Other settlers look after his wife and children, just as they will have to comfort them later in their grief. After the picnic, when the danger that Wilson poses is absolutely clear, Torrey still offers to accompany Shipstead to the blacksmith shop. 'A soldier who's fought in real battles', he will put on his thirty-eight and ride into town when he wants. When he finally faces Wilson, the two men are equally alone, each by his own choice. Wilson does not need the help of others. But Torrey does need help and he has cut himself off from it. Again and again he has chosen not to accept the consequences of belonging to something larger than himself, until he reaches the point where he can choose only to face his death.

When we meet Chris he adheres mindlessly to the rules of his group. Shane enters the bar room in clothes that mark him as a settler and no pig-farmer is going to trespass 'where the men are drinkin'. What Chris says is literally correct. We have already seen the bartender bring a flask out and pass it to Lewis, who does raise pigs. The cattlemen congratulate him when he thinks he has faced Shane down and they rally to avenge him in the first fist fight. But Chris does not stay to watch them beat up Shane.

The next three times we see Chris, he is completely silent. The first is during Torrey's funeral, which is not introduced with a conventional establishing shot of the cemetery or the mourners. Instead, Stevens begins the sequence with a dissolve from Martha and Fred Lewis on the porch of the house they are about to abandon, to the Ryker men. The 'Rykers' are

Torrey's burial

also on a porch, in front of Grafton's saloon. Chris is sitting at the left. During the dissolve he seems to take form out of Martha's skirt. The funeral party's distant 'Abide with Me' is the only sound. Chris leans forward and a cut presents him full face, fidgeting with his hands and glancing towards the Ryker brothers and Wilson. Another dissolve takes us to Cemetery Hill for the burial, with the town in the middle distance and the mountains far behind. By showing the Rykers first and featuring Chris, rather than immediately using the expected long shot of the funeral party, Stevens has changed a merely conventional transition into a wordless exposition of the moral problem that Chris is starting to face.

After the burial we see Chris again, in the same pose. He lowers his head as Ryker goes into the saloon laughing and does not follow the others into the bar. He is still on the porch when Ryker comes out to watch the settlers return to Lewis'. He hears the rancher say 'Starrett's holding them together'. We see him next inside the tavern, when Ryker is sending Morgan to lure Starrett to his death. Chris is hidden at first by the Ryker brothers. When they move, revealing him to the camera, Ryker greets him, 'Hello, Calloway'. He does not reply, but looks outside towards the departing 'peace party', whose murderous intention he knows.

His decision is made. He will abandon Ryker and warn Shane for Starrett's sake. One reason for not taking it to Starrett is that Joe will pay no heed. But Chris must also establish moral standing in the eyes of the man whom he thought he had shamed, but who had proven far better than he. Not an articulate man, he can only tell Shane that 'Somethin's come over me' and that he is moving on. His last words to Shane are 'Be seein' ya'. These are also the last words in *A Place in the Sun*, as the death row prisoners support George Eastman during his final walk. Unlike Torrey, who fails to carry through on his commitments, Chris has broken a commitment and in so doing has resolved his own tensions. Except for the few words that Chris exchanges with Shane, it is all shown by strictly cinematic means.

If we understand Wilson as overlapping with Torrey and Torrey with Chris, we can see Chris as sharing his dilemma with Shane, the ultimate outsider in this film. We do not even learn where he has come from. His answer to Joe's non-question – 'I wouldn't ask where you're bound' – is an uninformative 'one place or another, somewhere I've never been'. Marion 'think[s] we know' what drives Shane when he speaks to her of his own 'long story' after the farmers scorn him. One of the film's puzzles is what has driven a gunman like Shane to have even thought about going straight. It may be what he tells Ryker at the end: his time is over. Another, more dramatically satisfying explanation, can be teased out of the looks of pain that Ladd occasionally allows to pass over the character's face and out of the Calloway story. Chris may be Shane's inferior, but the search he is about to begin is like the one that brought Shane into the valley. The elimination of the sub-plot of the Lewis girl suggests that, like Shane's, it will have no end. Like the Ryker group, both might be doomed to remain men without women.

A woman's committed love may be what Shane thinks he wants (though not in the crass sense of having come to the valley just to get a woman). We have already noted his glance at Marion on his early line about going 'some place I've never been'. If he seeks love, his choice of the unreachable Marion suggests that something within him remains unsure. Marion appreciates that he will move on and she warns Joey against 'liking him too much'. It is not just Production Code conventions that prevent her from going off with him, or even just sleeping with him; it is that she is unattainable. This is completely understood throughout the film, despite their mutual attraction. Their sin, if sin it is, lies only in having desires to which neither can yield without violating their most basic beliefs and loyalties.

In this sense, Shane seems more than a little akin to Stevens himself, who also had a way of wanting to reconcile impossible contradictions. Though no longer married to the woman who bore his son, they remained close. Though he made the film as a testament against what he saw as a growing problem of firearms, he shared the American male interest in weaponry. Though the film is anti-gun, Shane's speech about a gun being as good or as bad as the man who uses it is essentially the argument put forward by the National Rifle Association. Though Stevens was far more a genuine Westerner than the Maine-born John Ford or the Ivy Leaguer Howard Hawks, he did not 'make Westerns'.

Shane squarely faces the dilemma posed by his irreconcilable desires. The time for gunfighting is over and he wants another life. Fate tempts him with an easy way to attain it: let Joe go. The code of independent male judgment requires that he do so. But doing the right thing requires that he break the rules of a fist fight, knock Joe out with his pistol and go himself. Marion understands this. His willingness to never

see her again represents the very most that he can do for her. All the things that he tells Joey as he is about to ride out of the valley and out of the child's life may be true. There is no living with a killer. A man has to be what he is. You cannot break the mould. He tried and it didn't work for him.

But Shane's real problem is not that he has killed. These killings could be justified, both under the law and within the Western genre's convention of town taming. What makes Shane a tragic character is his recognition that he cannot have all that he knows he wants. As much as Torrey's early bluster points towards his appointment with Wilson, Shane's earliest exchanges of glances with Marion requires that he eventually go back up the hill from which he first descended. When he came down, he entered a lush place of green plants and blue water, in broad daylight. When he leaves, spilled blood remains behind in the night.

He is wiser, though. So is the not-so-little boy who watches him go, though Joey's reverberating shouts of 'Mother wants you, I know she does', show that he has not grasped why Shane has to go. Shane must remain an outsider. The price of his staying would be too high and Joey would pay it. Stevens wanted to end *Alice Adams* with the central character understanding the implications of an adult choice, making that choice and accepting what it entailed. But studio power intervened and the film has instead a conventional happy ending. In *Shane*, both the 'Leatherstocking' convention that the wanderer be womanless and the great power that Stevens wielded allowed him to end the film the way that he wanted.

11
....

SHANE AND THE WESTERN GENRE

That *Shane's* apparent simplicity is highly deceptive, that its crafting and cinematic devices are complex and that Stevens knew exactly what he was doing throughout the production should be obvious. Why, however, does the film enjoy its continuing reputation as one of the premier Westerns? The problem presents no little irony. The other major film about end-of-the-frontier Wyoming is Michael Cimino's *Heaven's Gate*. Cimino shot it using the same technique of seemingly endless footage that Stevens employed. Yet this box-office and critical disaster has been widely blamed for the Western's virtual demise after its release in 1981.

Stevens and Paramount had their difficulties throughout the production, from initial correspondence to editing. At one point the studio nearly sold the film to Howard Hughes. None the less, Paramount gave *Shane* its full support on the film's release. Hollywood hype needs to be treated with caution, but the initial memo from the publicity office set the tone: '"Shane", George Stevens' great production is definitely Academy Award stature and should be so treated in carrying out all campaign ideas.' Fifty-nine different publicity stunts were suggested, including renaming Jackson Hole 'Shane' for a day and making Stevens its honorary mayor; starting a 'manhunt' for the elusive Jean Arthur and a 'clamour for a Pulitzer Prize to be awarded the best screenplay of the year'; working Victor Young's score into a symphonic suite (which did happen and has been recorded by the New Zealand Symphony Orchestra); and getting spots for Stevens on the *This is Your Life* or *You Asked for It* television programmes.

Stevens was a man of dignity and the reviews rendered such gimmicks unnecessary. The *New York Herald Tribune* called the film 'a superb Western and a first-rate motion picture'. Its reviewer understood Stevens' intention of treating a gun not as 'part of a costume, but a last, terrible resort' and of showing a gunman as 'a thing apart, an outcast with an unpleasant smell of death lingering about him'. For the *Daily News*, the film was 'a Western of unusual interest [with] an inspirational quality that raises it above the run-of-the-mill horse opera'. The *World-Telegram*, the *Post*, the *Daily Mirror*, the *Journal-American* and the *Brooklyn Eagle* all placed *Shane* among the top films of the genre, comparing it with *High Noon*, *Stagecoach*, *The Covered Wagon* and *Red River*. According to the *Mirror*'s reviewer *Shane* was 'the best Western saga of all time'. The *Post* called it '"only a Western" in the sense that "Romeo and Juliet" is "only a love story"'. Alton Cook wrote in the *World-Telegram*, 'In his very first Western film, Stevens has stepped right into the ranks of top masters of the craft.'

Bosley Crowther of *The New York Times* was equally enthusiastic. He too compared it to *High Noon* and thought it scarcely 'possible that the screen should so soon again come up with another great Western film. Yet, that is substantially what has happened in the case of George Stevens' "Shane".' Alone among the New York reviewers, Crowther caught the influence of Remington, Russell and the other painters whom Stevens had studied. But he barely grasped Stevens' concern about weapons, noting merely that the film 'contains a disturbing revelation of the savagery that prevailed in the hearts of the old gun-fighters, who were simply legal killers under the frontier code'.

The trade reviews were similarly complimentary. *Motion Picture Herald* called *Shane* 'an achievement in the cinematic art of the like of which showmen have rarely seen ... an achievement the artistic success of which in no way interferes with an enormous box office potential [a]nd ... a superlative personal achievement by George Stevens'. *Film Bulletin* likened *Shane* to *Stagecoach*. So did *The Morning Telegraph*, adding *High Noon* and *The Gunfighter* to the list and suggesting that 'it may very well be the best Western the movies have made in years'. For *Motion Picture Daily* the Western genre was not large enough to offer an adequate comparison and cited *Gone With the Wind* as one possible comparison: 'Make way now for one of the great ones. One of the great ones of the screen's first half-century.' *Showmen's Trade Review* noted that '"Shane" replaces "The Covered Wagon", "Stagecoach" and other past Western epics as the target for future producers to surpass, for it is undoubtedly the best Western ever made'. In its inimitable style, *Variety* called it a 'socko drama of the West that ... is by no means a conventional giddyap feature in Technicolor'.

Except for Bosley Crowther, who chose *Shane* as one of only two
Westerns among his fifty *Great Films* (1967), latter-day critics and scholars
have not been so kind. As early as 1954 Robert Warshow suggested that
Shane's 'aestheticizing tendency', its fairy-tale 'dreamy clarity', and its
attempt 'to freeze the Western myth once and for all' were flaws rather than
achievements. In 1968 in *The American Cinema*, Andrew Sarris excluded
Stevens from his 'pantheon directors', as merely 'the master of the slow
dissolve'. Leo Braudy and Morris Dickstein did not include him in their
anthology *Great Film Directors* (1978). Pauline Kael wrote that
'superficially, this is a Western, but from Shane's knightly costume, from
the way his horse canters, from the Agincourt music, it's all too
recognizable as an attempt to create a myth. . . . This George Stevens film is
over-planned and uninspired; Westerns are better when they're not so
self-importantly self-conscious.' Brian Garfield agreed: 'Shane may well
be the ultimate expression of the Western legend, but the film does have
flaws' [including] 'self conscious Myth . . . something too studied about the
panoramic imagery . . . the black costume worn by Palace.' Since Garfield
incorrectly included Lee van Cleef in the cast, his failure to note that only
Wilson's hat is black makes one doubt that he watched the movie closely.
(So does Robert Warshow's comment that Shane 'emerges mysteriously
from the plains', when in fact he comes from the mountains.)

Jane Tompkins is also critical. She does stress the film's significance
in her *West of Everything* (1992), but she sees the enraged Marion's
verbal savaging of Joe's frontier dream as mere words. Missing Stevens'
intention, Richard Slotkin sees as the 'underlying message' of the
narrative the idea that 'a "good man with a gun" is in every sense the best
of men – an armed redeemer who is the sole vindicator of the "liberties
of the people", the "indispensable man" in the quest for progress'. Most
recently, the literary scholar Joseph M. Flora describes the problems the
film poses for a late-twentieth century teacher. In 1993 'the reaction [to a
student screening] was mainly negative. There were many laughs that
director Stevens had not intended. The only part . . . the class liked was
Jack Palance's performance. Brandon de Wilde as young "Joey" . . . was
especially vulnerable to criticism'. 'He's such a whiner,' one student
complained. Flora's students also thought Schaefer's novel belonged 'in
junior high and that it was not worth their time'.

People who have faced the creative task of writing and making
Westerns have been a great deal more appreciative. Flora cites actor

Anthony Hopkins and novelist Larry Brown as both being deeply influenced by the film. As already noted, Clint Eastwood's *Pale Rider* is a *Shane* remake, even to the extent of naming its Joe Starrett figure 'Hull Barrett'. (It is a mark of changed times that Eastwood's own Shane figure has his way sexually both with Barrett's wife and, for good measure, with the Barretts' grown-up daughter, who replaces the character of Joey.) Warren Beatty drew on the Stevens howitzer technique for gunshots in *Bonnie and Clyde*. He tells with amusement of realising that the sound levels were all wrong during a London screening and of having the projectionist explain that he had worked out a chart so that he could raise and lower the volume, because this was the 'worst mixed' movie he had projected 'since *Shane*'. Though George Stevens did not study other film-makers, they have studied him.

Perhaps Stevens' most noteworthy student was Sam Peckinpah. According to Peckinpah's astute critic Paul Seydor, the director's

> [M]ost dramatic stylistic innovation – that combination of fast cutting and slow motion to render violence – was suggested by . . . George Stevens, whose *Shane* Peckinpah once called 'the best Western ever made,' to which remark he some years later added: 'Killing used to be fun-and-games in Apache land. Violence wasn't shown well. You fired a shot and three Indians fell down. You always expected them to get up again. But when Jack Palance shot Elisha Cook, Jr, in *Shane*, things started to change.'

Seydor goes on to demonstrate how the killing of Wilson 'appears from our present vantage point, to be a remarkable adumbration of Peckinpah. When Shane draws and fires . . . it is with lightning speed and over in a split second. The recoil, however, is protracted, as Wilson's body takes the bullet, is thrown across the length of the bar room, crashes through some tables and chairs and lands in the corner dead.' Whatever the controversy around Peckinpah's depiction of violence, his intention can be seen as similar to Stevens', when he wired Elisha Cook Jr and jerked him into the mud. Both directors wanted to show the damage that bullets can do to people.

That, however, does not exhaust the topic. Stevens used no exploding bags of chicken blood or intercut slow motion. By Peckinpah standards his cutting seems positively slow. As noted, there are only four set-ups in the entire Torrey killing. Stevens did use very fast cutting during the first fight, however, particularly after Joe enters the bar room to rescue Shane from the Rykers. One shot in particular points directly towards the Peckinpah subjective hand-held camera technique. This captures Joe filling the screen as he charges Ryker with an axe-handle. We see the shot through Ryker's suddenly frightened eyes. It is striking enough seen on a television screen or with a 16mm projection. Its original effect in Radio City Music Hall can only be imagined.

There is at least one other moment at which Stevens' influence on the Peckinpah style seems palpable. Near the end of *The Wild Bunch*, Peckinpah builds tension to an almost intolerable level as his protagonists push their way through a thick crowd of Mexican extras. The shot combines a very slow zoom and backward track to fill the screen with the four gunmen, who are on their way to their own Armageddon. Stevens also used the technique of an action emerging from deep within the frame and displacing what is in the foreground, especially to set up Torrey's killing, when Wilson takes a slow and menacing walk towards the camera along the porch in front of Grafton's. If Peckinpah admired the Stevens film as much as he said, the inspiration for his own remarkable composition when death walks out of the depths of the screen seems clear.

How does *Shane* fare now, forty-six years after its release? Audience response at student screenings may suggest that its resurrection has yet to come. But continuing admiration of the film by film-makers suggests that they have appreciated what George Stevens put into the film, in terms both of what he had to say and of how he said it. Moreover, the film has a place among the few Westerns listed on three contemporary best films lists: the National Film Directory of the Library of Congress, the Arts and Entertainment Network's 'Monthly Guide to the Best Movies Ever Made' and 'Videohound's 125 Best Movies' as well, of course, as the BFI list of classics. Works of art do fall out of fashion, only to receive fresh appreciation at a later date. Perhaps *Shane* will come back in critical and popular appreciation. Among film-makers who have come after Stevens, as among the earlier film-makers who worked with him, that appreciation never went away.

CREDITS

· ·

Shane

USA
1952
US Release
24 April 1953
Distributor
Paramount Pictures
Corporation
British Release
26 October 1953

Copyright Date
1952

Production Company
Paramount Pictures
Corporation
Producer
George Stevens
Associate Producer
Ivan Moffat
Assistant to Producer
Howie Horwiz
Director
George Stevens
Associate Director
Fred Guiol
Assistant Director
John Coonan
Screenplay
A.B. Guthrie Jr
Based on the novel by
Jack Schaefer
Additional Dialogue
Jack Sher
Director of Photography
Loyal Griggs
**2nd Unit Director of
Photography**
Irmin Roberts
Colour Consultant
Richard Mueller
**Special Photographic
Effects**
Gordon Jennings
Process Photography
Farciot Edouart

Editors
William Hornbeck,
Tom McAdoo
Art Directors
Hal Pereira, Walter Tyler
Set Decorator
Emile Kuri
Costumes
Edith Head
Make-up Supervisor
Wally Westmore
Music
Victor Young
Sound
Harry Lindgren,
Gene Garvin
Technical Adviser
Joe De Yong

Cast
Alan Ladd
Shane
Jean Arthur
Marion Starrett
Van Heflin
Joe Starrett
Brandon De Wilde
Joey Starett
Walter Jack Palance
Jack Wilson
Ben Johnson
Chris Calloway
Edgar Buchanan
Fred Lewis
Emile Meyer
Rufus Ryker
Elisha Cook Jr
Stonewall Torrey
Douglas Spencer
Axel Shipstead
John Dierkes
Morgan Ryker
Ellen Corby
Mrs Torrey
Paul McVey
Sam Grafton
John Miller
Atkey

Edith Evanson
Mrs Shipstead
Leonard Strong
Ernie Wright
Ray Spiker
Johnson
Janice Carroll
Susan Lewis
Martin Mason
Howells
Helen Brown
Martha Lewis
Nancy Kulp
Mrs Howells

[and uncredited]
Howard J. Negley
Pete
Beverly Washburn
Ruth Lewis
George J. Lewis
Jack Sterling
Henry Wills
Rex Moore
Ewing Brown
Chester W. Hannan
Bill Cartledge
Steve Raines
Ryker men
Charles Quirk
clerk

10,600 feet
118 minutes

Colour by
Technicolor

Credits compiled by
Markku Salmi,
BFI Filmographic Unit

BIBLIOGRAPHY

. . . .

George Stevens' films remain almost untouched by either scholarship or criticism. The only biography is the film account by his son George Stevens Jr, *George Stevens: A Filmmaker's Journey* (1985). One short book and two theses attempt overviews of his work. The book is Donald Richie, *George Stevens: An American Romantic* (New York: Museum of Modern Art, 1970); the theses are Bruce Petri, 'A Theory of American Film: The Films and Techniques of George Stevens' (Ph.D., Harvard University, 1974) and John A. Todd, 'The Films, Life, and Times of George Stevens' (M.S., Boston University, 1996).

The enormous George Stevens archive at the Margaret Herrick Library of the Academy of Motion Picture Arts and Sciences still awaits exploration, let alone full scholarly exploitation. Quotations from film-industry figures (except Sam Peckinpah and Ben Johnson) regarding Stevens and his work, and from Stevens himself, are taken from the Stevens archive, as are quotations from drafts of the script, other production material and promotional material. The Peckinpah quotations are from Paul Seydor, *Peckinpah: The Western Films* (Urbana: University of Illinois Press, 1980). Ben Johnson material is derived from the interview transcript in the Oral History of American Performing Arts collection at Southern Methodist University. Quotations from George Stevens Jr are taken from an interview taped in 1994 in Washington, D.C. and from correspondence regarding drafts of the manuscript.

Cheap editions of the Jack Schaefer novel are readily found, but James C. Work has edited a critical edition (Lincoln: University of Nebraska Press, 1994) that includes interviews, scholarship and criticism. It also reprints several reviews of the film and includes essays by James K. Folsom, Michael T. Marsden and Harry Schein. Most coffee table books on the Westerns deal with *Shane*, but they are usually so bereft of either scholarship or intelligent criticism that they do not bear listing. One exception is Bosley Crowther's *The Great Films* (New York: Putnam, 1967) which has an appreciative and insightful essay-length review. Among academic accounts, Will Wright devotes considerable attention to *Shane* in *Sixguns and Society: A Structural Study of the Western* (Berkeley: University of California Press, 1975), treating it as an important exemplar of what he calls 'the classical plot'. Two major books published in 1992 examine *Shane* in the course of more extended treatments of the Western genre. The first is Jane P. Tompkins, *West of Everything: The Inner Life of Westerns* (New York: Oxford University Press); the second is Richard Slotkin, *Gunfighter Nation: The Myth of the Frontier in Twentieth-Century America* (New York: Atheneum), which treats the film as an uncritical exemplar of the mid-century 'cult of the gunfighter'. More recently, Michael Coyne stresses the theme of family dysfunction within *Shane* in *The Crowded Prairie: American National Identity in the Hollywood Western* (London: I. B. Tauris, 1997).

The best introduction to the genre as a whole is Edward Buscombe's 'The Western: A Short History' in *The BFI Companion to the Western* (London: Andre Deutsch, 1988). More recently Buscombe and Roberta E. Pearson have collaborated to edit *Back in the Saddle Again: New Essays on the Western* (London: BFI Publishing, 1998).

Chuck Rankin's 'Clash of Frontier: A Historical Parallel to Jack Schaefer's *Shane*' introduces the real events of the Johnson County, Wyoming, range wars. The essay appears in Work's critical edition of *Shane*. Historian Frederick Jackson Turner first delivered his 'Frontier Thesis' ('The Significance of the Frontier in American History') at the American Historical Association convention in Chicago, 1893. Turner's argument has generated an enormous body of scholarly debate that continues to the present day. The most recent summary is Richard Etulain, ed., *Historians at Work: Did the Frontier Experience Make America Exceptional* (Boston: Bedford/St. Martin's, 1999), which contains Turner's original text. See also Henry Nash Smith, *Virgin Land: The American West as Symbol and Myth* (Cambridge: Harvard University Press, 1950) and Richard White and Patricia Nelson Limerick, *The Frontier in American Culture* (Berkeley: University of California Press, 1994). Richard White's *It's Your Misfortune and None of My Own: A History of the American West* (Norman: University of Oklahoma Press, 1991) has replaced Ray Allen Billington, *Westward Expansion: A History of the American Frontier* (New York: Macmillan, 1949) as the standard overview. Edward Countryman's *Americans: A Collision of Histories* (New York: Hill & Wang, 1996) addresses the problems of American historical identity that are central to *Shane*.

ALSO PUBLISHED

If you would like further information about future BFI Film Classics or about other books on film, media and popular culture from BFI Publishing, please write to:

BFI Film Classics
BFI Publishing
21 Stephen Street
London W1P 2LN